RIPPLES: STORIES OF ADDICTION

RECOVERY IS POSSIBLE

PATRICIA GREENE

© **Copyright 2023 - All rights reserved.**

The content contained within this book may not be reproduced, duplicated, or transmitted without direct written permission from the author or the publisher.

Under no circumstances will any blame or legal responsibility be held against the publisher, or author, for any damages, reparation, or monetary loss due to the information contained within this book, either directly or indirectly.

Legal Notice:

This book is copyright protected. It is only for personal use. You cannot amend, distribute, sell, use, quote, or paraphrase any part, or the content within this book, without the author or publisher's permission.

Disclaimer Notice:

Please note that the information contained within this document is for educational and entertainment purposes only. All effort has been executed to present accurate, up-to-date, reliable, complete information. No warranties of any kind are declared or implied. Readers acknowledge that the author is not rendering legal, financial, medical, or professional advice. The content within this book has been derived from various sources. Please consult a licensed professional before attempting any techniques outlined in this book.

By reading this document, the reader agrees that under no circumstances is the author responsible for any losses, direct or indirect, that are incurred due to the use of the information in this document, including, but not limited to, errors, omissions, or inaccuracies.

For my granddaughter Joely
Who has put up with all my ups and downs,
always knew just the right thing to say when I would get frustrated.
To love me unconditional. (which is a challenge at times)
I love you to the moon and back

For my Fur babies
Riley, Coco, Oscar, Peanut, Bobby and Miley
Who sat under my desk, licked my toes, steal my sandwich, kept a keen eye of my every move, but never left my side.

For all my grandchildren who are my love and life line
You know I do this for you
Cami, Wesley, Bree
Esme
Levi, Meredith
Kiyah

My beloved mother Boots, you always told me I could do anything

CONTENTS

Foreword — 7
Introduction — 9

Part I
LOSS
"Nathaniel Poirier" — 19
"Negative Influences of a Positive Man v2.0" — 33
"Strength Is What We Gain from The Madness We Survive" — 47
"Addiction is not a character flaw" — 55

Part II
RECOVERY IS POSSIBLE
Recovery — 63
"Billy and Harley" — 65
"The Stigma of Addiction" — 73
"From out of the shadows she walks like a dream" — 91
"Can We Skip to The Good Part?" — 95
"Mission Impossible" — 123
"Monsters are real and they're trained how to kill" — 151
"Ms. Annie Lehman" — 169

PART III
From Addict to Addiction Professional — 191
LEADING THROUGH ADVERSITY — 207
Prepared by: W. Todd Catalgarone Sheriff of Elk County

References — 219
"Substance Use Disorder Respects No One" — 221

"A Pharmacists Journey of Understanding Opioid Use Disorder"	225
"The Last Step"	235
Final Thoughts	239
I want to Thank	247

FOREWORD

Human beings can become addicted to a variety of substances or behaviors. Street drugs and alcohol are the most commonly known and abused, but there are numerous other addictions that can take control of a person's life, such as pain medication, nicotine, caffeine, chocolate, video games, gambling, shopping, eating, plastic surgery, and sex to name a few.

The vast scope of addictive behaviors, along with the devastation that addiction causes in our lives, is why it is so important to focus on the causes of, and possible cures for addiction. At the same time, it is important to give special priority to drug and alcohol misuse, because substance abuse disorders are often the most destructive of all our addictions.

Any substance or activity that causes mood changes in an individual can be addictive. The substance or activity of choice becomes a form of self-medication that eventually gets out of control.

In the end, it's up to the individual to want to regain control of their life before effective changes and healing can take place. There are various methods that we try to treat addictions: education, support groups, interventions, incarcerations, and rehabilitations, long and short term. In short, rewards and punishments, or behavior modification programs can all be of help. However, the success of any treatment is determined by the individual's desire to change, their own, personal endurance and determination, and a great deal of support for the addict to begin to heal and resolve the problem. Treatment isn't a one shoe fits all. Often, an individual may try several forms of treatments in order to finally help themselves to overcome their addiction.

What doesn't work is ignoring the problem in hopes that it will just go away. If your loved one is addicted, you need to address it, but not by nagging, bargaining, and complaining. Most addicts grow numb to such onslaughts. Pretending there isn't a problem will solve nothing. It is important to try to understand their dilemma, and show that you care.

~ **Steve Gibbs**

INTRODUCTION

"Why can't they just stop?"

"They know it's killing them, so? Just stop!"

"Don't they care what they are doing to their family, the people who love them? "

"Narcan? They abuse it, they should be left to die".

"All druggies are losers!"

How many of you have said this about people stuck in the world of addiction?

Why? Because you don't understand their world, or you have never had a loved one stuck there.

INTRODUCTION

I remember one time I had planned a Narcan training. This was way before it was so easily available for people. I knew so many families who worried all the time about coming home to find their loved one had overdosed. So, when Narcan came out, I thought, "wow, maybe this can save someone and give them one more chance to get clean." Maybe this could stop the heartache I had suffered.

As I walked away that night from the meeting feeling very positive, I ran into an old friend. They asked me what was I up to, and I explained that I was trying to get a Narcan training together.

The reply is burned into my heart, "Why? I think if they overdose that is their fault. I believe we should just let them die." I felt like a dagger went through my heart. They knew Danny, they knew he died. But I think for that split second, they forgot and their true feelings came out. I stopped in my tracks and said, "Until it is someone you love, your child, your grandchild. Then you would think differently." I believe that is when they remembered that Danny had passed from an overdose. But those words were bitter and hard for me to swallow. Now every time I see that person, I hear those words. The thing is, I would never in a million years have expected such a thing coming from them.

What that conversation told me was that people really don't understand the world of addiction. Not just for the addict, but for the people who love them who have to stand by and watch.

INTRODUCTION

So, in this book, my plan is to open the eyes of those who think, "We should just let them die." I want people to see that the world is not black and white, or even grey. I hope that they will see the world of addiction as the addict does, as the people who love the addict do, and as professionals who work with the addict see it every day.

I have spent hours talking to many of the people who contributed to this book, trying to gain their perspective. I have also talked to people who have allowed the stigma to silence them because they are afraid of what you might think of them.

I know one thing for sure, we keep dumping money and energy into programs and we have still made so little progress. I don't know what the answer is, I still just have a whole lot of questions.

I hate to say that our system is broken, because I really do believe that they try. I just have to ask that, if this isn't working, what can we do to fix it? What can we do to make our system work, and help the people who are suffering?

I am so sick of watching the struggles people have when looking for help for their loved ones. I am so sick of hearing how another young life was taken by this monster of addiction. Every time I hear another one has died, I feel the pain of that mother, father, and family. I hear the million questions they are asking themselves; *"What could I have done differently?" "If I would have only been home earlier,"* and, *"Why?"*

INTRODUCTION

Out of all the questions that rattle around in our heads, that "WHY?" screams the loudest.

As you read these stories, you will find that many of the victims had normal childhoods, parents at home, Sunday dinners, Christmases with the grandparents. What was going on inside these kids? What broke them? Where did they disappear to? What happened to drive them to enter that dark world of addiction?

I have heard from so many people trying in some way to make sense out of the addict's choices. Often, they try to convince themselves;

"They didn't love us enough!"; "They don't care about themselves!"; "They are selfish!"; "They need to hit rock bottom!"; "Tough love is the answer!"

What? Well, let me tell you what. Rock bottom, for some, is 6 feet under, or they sit on your shelf in a little box. The same can happen with tough love. Turning your back on someone that is already full of shame and guilt is not love. I'm not saying to hand over the keys to the house or the pin number to your bank account. I'm just saying that "tough love" often turns them cold and makes them feel even more alone.

You will read all about rock bottom in the stories of recovery. Hopefully, the stories will help you to find more understanding. or they may lead you to ask a whole lot of questions. Either way, it is a step in the right direction; a conversation about a subject that has been swept under the

INTRODUCTION

rug, hidden behind closed doors, and just plain ignored. After all, not my child, right?

I have one more story I would like to share.

UNDER THE BRIDGE

A few years back I took a bunch of stuff down to Pittsburgh. I had tents, blankets, clothes, coats, socks, hand warmers and food. I was to meet up with a friend of mine who helps the homeless there who live under a bridge. It was just one group of many that she would check in on, and help out as much as she could.

Once we arrived there, we were met by an elderly man I will call Joe, and he was in pretty good spirits. Joe was the guy who would check in on the people who lived under the bridge. He had just recently got his first apartment because he had also lived under the bridge for many years. Joe told me that it was an adjustment for him, that he was used to living out in the open and sleeping under the stars. Yes, he liked having warm water, a bed and all the other stuff, but there was something that would pull him back there, and he would spend the night with the rest of them sometimes.

Joe helped us unload the car with the stuff we had brought for them. As I looked around, my heart fell. These were young men and women, maybe 19 to 23 years old. Sleeping on old couches and using clothes as blankets. There were a couple of small tents there, I looked in to see a young man

INTRODUCTION

sleeping on top of a heap of his belongings for a make shift bed. The old couch and chairs were around a fire pit. But, what hit me the hardest was the young man sitting on the couch. He was just sitting there staring into the fire; no emotions, no facial expressions. I looked at him and handed him some stuff and said hello. He never looked up, but instead, popped open a can of beer that was sitting there. I tried again to talk to him, he looked like he couldn't be very old. His eyes were hollow, and I felt such sadness. This young man was lost in his world; was there someone looking for him? Or was he someone who had slipped through the cracks, someone who nobody cared about anymore? My heart hurt, and I knew if I kept watching I would surely start to cry.

Joe called him by name and the man looked up at him. That was about all that he could do. Joe shrugged his shoulders, letting me know that this is how it is out here. Then Joe told me that they used to have a port-a-potty, but some kids came up and knocked it over while one of the guys was in it. In fact, they did this several times, so the city took it away. With no toilet, they would just go around the corner, behind of one of the pillars of the bridge for some privacy. It didn't make any sense to me how people could be so cruel.

I noticed a box of food sitting there that contained moldy bread, and very ripe veggies and fruit. One of the local stores had left it for the group earlier that day. Joe said that they were happy to have it! Coming from a small town, it was

INTRODUCTION

hard for me to wrap my head around this. I thought all of that was sad enough, and then Joe told me that he had come up to check on the boys one day and found someone laying by the fire, dead. He had frozen sometime during the night. My mind was swirling; how does this happen? **Why** does this happen?

So, that brings me back to this "rock bottom." Please explain to me what is rock bottom? Because I sure as heck don't know.

I have since talked to many others who have told me stories about living in what they call "crack houses," and what they had to do to survive there. And, that still wasn't a rock bottom.

I hope the stories in this book open your eyes. I hope that you share them with your children, and that you have those tough conversations about addiction. Nobody is immune to it; not you, not me, and not our younger generation. We are losing so many of our loved ones at such an alarming rate. How do we stop it? It is said that when we know better we do better, so what is the answer?

The best that I know right now is to stop hiding from it. We must talk about it, talk about it again, and never stop talking about it. We must help everyone to "know better." Most of all...

WE MUST STOP THE STIGMA...

PART I

LOSS

In one swift moment in time
Our world changed forever
Now we have to learn to live
Without you here

"NATHANIEL POIRIER"

1981 – 2021

He was a son; He was a brother. He was a nephew; he was an uncle. He was a grandson; he was a great grandson. He was so funny; he was so soft hearted. He was a drug addict. He was loved.

Nat's journey into this world started on Monday, September 24, 1984. Sixteen minutes after his older brother. (I would tell him all the time that is why he always wanted five more minutes of sleep.) In addition to his twin brother, Nat also has another brother who was five years older.

As my boys grew, Nat was always the follower. In preschool his teacher would tell me how he always waited for his brother to start his papers before Nat would start his own. In elementary school, I had them separated as much as possible, but in a small school, their friends were the same set of boys.

Nat was the target of a lot of teasing. A major reason was that he had red hair. Neither my husband nor I had red hair, but both of his grandmothers did. In addition to his read hair, he seemed learn slower than his brother which often made him frustrated and angry.

When he was ten, his father had a heart attack and very nearly died. He survived and recovered from lifesaving surgery. The trauma of his dad's heart attack changed Nat. His Dad had a few scary visits to the hospital, and every time he came home, Nat became a different person. He would often get into verbal and physical altercations with his brothers. He would cry easily, and his behavior got out of control. We took him to his doctor who suggested a therapist. Nat was prescribed an antidepressant and that seemed to help.

When he started middle school, Nat seemed to do a little better. It was easier to keep him separated from his brother, now. He joined the basketball team, but again he did not excel, got frustrated, and quit. Years later I found out that he would skip practice and go smoke pot. I guess that was why he did not excel at basketball.

Nat's friends started to change from his and Nick's friends to just his friends. We found out later that there were two reasons for this, one being that he was tired of having the same friends as his brother. The second reason was that this new set of friends were also into the "pot thing"

Going into high school, he still faced struggles with learning, but managed to pass with low grades. For the most part, his high school years seemed normal. He dated a few girls and got into trouble by skipping school a few times. The summer before his junior year, he and his brother started working at a little secondary shop. They turned eighteen right after the senior year began. Nat got into a little trouble with the law, mostly speeding tickets, that sort of thing. He still dated a few girls but nothing serious. The girls loved him because he was so soft hearted and eager to please and would always agree to take them where they wanted to go.

Near the end of his senior year, he surprised us by telling us he wanted to continue his education and go to school to be a machinist. He applied and was accepted at ITEC, in Ridgway. He started a job working third shift, so that he could go to school during the day from 8-4pm. Then, he would come home, eat, sleep, and start all over. Two weeks after school started on his 19th birthday, Nat's best friend was killed in a car accident. He was asked to be a pallbearer, and he deeply mourned his friend. According to Nat, this was his very first friend that was just his friend, not both his and Nick's friend.

Nat's schooling required so many hours and they were very strict with students. Since he went straight from school to work, we were unaware that he started missing several days. Instead of going to class, he would go somewhere and smoke pot. We only found out because the director of his school called to warn us that he may not graduate because of so much missed time. One night, Nat did not come home to sleep or eat, and had still not shown up by the time he would have had to go to work. We searched everywhere, even called the police for them to be on the lookout for him. We found him at a known drug dealer's house, dragged him out of there, and took him to school.

When school was done for the day, we picked him up and had a little talk with him. Not that it did much good. He had been fired from work for absenteeism, and his schooling was in jeopardy.

Eventually, he graduated with a degree in machining and was so proud of himself. We felt that his life was finally going to be normal. He got a job in Dubois, lost his job in Dubois, and then had various other jobs that he lost because he didn't show up. He moved out and into a trailer not far from our house. I begged him not to, I even called the landlord and begged him not to rent to him. But he moved anyway and shortly after, got his first DUI. Nat got his second DUI about six months later, and ended up spending Easter weekend in jail.

Not long after his second DUI, he was put in jail for parole violation and while he was there, he allowed us to move him back home. For a small period of time, he became a new person. He had a full-time girlfriend and again we felt that maybe his life was going in the right direction. He was clean and sober, and started a new job that he really liked, and that he actually showed up for.

Life, again, threw us all a curve. Nat's father died on New Year's Day following complications from triple bypass surgery. The whole family was in shock. We all pretty much shut down. However, after about six months our lives started to become somewhat normal again. Nat and his girlfriend found an apartment and moved in together. I was okay with it, not 100% okay, but okay with it. Between her family and mine, we helped furnish the apartment and make it nice for them.

Again, life interfered, and Nat had been having back issues, so he went to a doctor. He found out that he had a cyst on his back that was the size of a golf ball. Surgery was required, and he missed some work. Nat started with pain pills and ended up with a lot more drugs. During this time, I learned that he had no money. Most went for drugs, and some for food, but he and his girlfriend often ordered out, so food was pricey.

Then they started fighting all the time, and she ended up asking him to leave the apartment. My brother and I moved him home once again. Unfortunately, his drug use continued. Nat stole from me and he stole from his grandmother. When Nat met with his probation officer shortly after, he was found to have drugs in his system. They put him in county jail for 3 months and when he came out, he went to his first rehab. By this time, his relationship with his brothers had disappeared. They were angry at him and me. Somehow, they felt that I should have been able to control his drug habit.

After rehab, Nat was clean, but only for a short period of time. The next time that he had drugs in his system during his visit to his probation officer, they sent him to state prison. What an awful time that was! When I went to visit, I was always alone because his brothers no longer supported him. I would cry, then he would cry, and then he would be mad because I made him cry. It was also scary. Nat would tell me about things happening in the prison and I would fear for his safety.

When his time was up, I picked him up and off he went to yet another rehab. The pattern of rehab, short lived sobriety, using, rehab, short lived sobriety and using, would continue for a while. Sometimes when he was using, I would have no idea if he was dead or alive. Often, during sober times, I would help him set up an apartment, only for him to lose it for non-payment of rent, or he went to jail again.

During Nat's second time in state prison, my mother was diagnosed with lung cancer and given only a few months to live, and his twin brother's wedding was coming up. He was not invited to the wedding because of being in prison. I had taken my mother to see him in prison because she was doing so badly, and I worried she would pass before seeing him again. When she passed two months after her diagnosis, I could have brought him home for twelve hours, but it would have cost a large amount of money. Nat would only be allowed to go to the funeral home alone with the guard that came with him, and then return to the prison. My mother was cremated, so having him come home was really not an option. Thankfully, she got to see him before she passed. Two weeks after we buried her, I walked down the aisle at my son's wedding with a bittersweet heart. My son was marrying his sweetheart, but his dad, his grandmother and his twin brother were not there.

After Nat was released from state prison, he came home and repeated the cycle of sobriety, job, relapse, rehab. He went through a period of major depression while trying to beat his addiction. Twice he tried to kill himself and was admitted to a mental health facility. Medicine would help, but before long, he would forget to take it, or decide that he did not need it.

Nat had joined Narcotics Anonymous (NA) and went to meetings regularly. There, he met some awesome people who supported and encouraged him. One person became his sponsor, and it was truly wonderful for him. His sponsor would come to the house and would take Nat to meetings out of town, and encourage him to work on his twelve steps. Also, during this time, his older brother divorced and found a new girlfriend, and he and Nat reunited. Even though Nat was not in town and had not met his brother's new wife, he welcomed her in a text.

When Nat came home to live with me for what became the last time, he was able to reconnect with his nephew and his niece, and connect with his new step-nephew and step-niece. They all loved him, and he lectured them often about the dangers and consequences of drug use.

Despite the love Nat now received from his family, he still struggled with his addiction, and finally decided that he could no longer live in this area. So, he went to another rehab and upon completing his 28 days, went to Butler to live in a halfway house. That was two days before Christmas of 2020.

Even though we did not see him for Christmas, we all felt better about him because he had a better attitude and seemed happy. Nat then relapsed and returned to rehab for a short period of time, and then returned to stay at his halfway house.

Nat got a job that he liked, but after about a month found one that he liked better. He was finally going to be working as a machinist. He loved his new job and he loved his house. Nat became good friends with someone he met at rehab and who had moved to Butler around the same time as he had. They spent a lot of time together going to meetings, and working at the same job.

Nat had decided to move to a different house and was having some difficulty finding a new one. Then he told me that he had found a new place, and he moved in.

The day before Mother's Day, May 8, 2021, my oldest son was having me to his house for brunch. They were going to Buffalo, New York on Mother's Day to get a new puppy. When I got to my son's house, no one was home. He sent me a text saying he would be there shortly. So, I sat in my car reading some emails, and looked up and saw Nat. I jumped out of the car and gave him a big hug. I was so happy to see him. We hugged and I cried, and he cried. When I asked him why he was crying, he said because I was. I just kept hugging him. Soon my son came home, and we had an awesome brunch with Nat keeping us laughing telling his usual stories.

When we left my older son's house, Nat came to my house for a few minutes before he left to go back to Butler. I had promised to work a few hours that day so that another woman could work and not be alone. I left for work and Nat left to go back up to his brother's house. When I came home from work, there was candy and some other groceries. Nat felt that I did not have enough food in my house, so he had gone shopping and bought a ton of stuff for me: chicken, bread, peanut butter, hamburgers, all sorts of things. When I talked to him, he told me that he did not want me to not have things to eat.

Every night after that, Nat called me either on his first break or his second break. On Thursday, May 13, he did not call me. At first, I wondered why, but then remembered that Thursdays were his last day of the week for work. He worked 10-hour shifts, so often he would call me after work, or not until Friday, because he was so tired.

That morning, I went to Irwin to see my other son, daughter-in-law and 4-year-old granddaughter. I was working three days a week and laid of two days a week.

RIPPLES: STORIES OF ADDICTION

"The phone call no parent ever wants"

Friday morning around 8:30 my phone rang, and it was a Butler number. It was not Nat. The voice on the other end asked if I was Nathaniel Poirier's mother, and when he said that he hated to tell this to me on the phone, I knew. He told me that Nat had passed away the night before. His official time of death was 11:31p.m. MY life as I had known it ended at that moment.

Nat had told me various times during his sober periods that he absolutely hated being an addict. He hoped that, someday, he would either be able to become a drug counselor, or go into schools and tell them the real story of addiction. He hoped that he may be able to save one person from that kind of hell here on earth. The next day I received this text from Nat's good friend:

"Hello this is Nick. I was in Alpine Springs with Nat in November/December. He was my best and truest friend since I started this journey in recovery. I worked with him at Adams, we went to meetings, I took him to reptile expos, etc....I just wanted to reach out and offer my deepest sympathy for your loss. I recently achieved 6 months clean, and I wanted you to know that your son is a huge reason why. He helped me in countless ways. The most important being that he was a selfless and genuinely altruistic person who helped me with rides when I had no car, food when I had nothing to eat, and an ear when I had no one to talk to. I loved

your son as a brother. I haven't cried since I got clean until yesterday... I know you are overwhelmed and busy but I would like to attend any services that might be taking place. Any info would be much appreciated. I am sorry, again. God bless. Without Nat, I wouldn't be where I am today."

So, my son helped more than he knew, and I am eternally grateful to Nick for reaching out. He spoke at Nat's funeral.

It took a few days for Nat's autopsy to be completed, and then the following Wednesday, we said goodbye to my son. It is one of life's most heart wrenching times when they close that lid on your child's casket, and you know that is the last time you will see him.

His toxicology report came back indicating that he had passed as a result of meth, fentanyl, and heroin. His death was ruled accidental. The Attorney General has his 'phone in hopes that they can find who sold him the drugs, and prosecute them for murder.

Now my son's tombstone will read:

"I am free, I have followed the path that God has planned for me."

He was my son. He was my sons' brother. He was my parent's grandson. He was my grandchildren's uncle. He was my brother's nephew. He was so kind, so funny. He was so soft hearted. He was a machinist. He was a drug addict.

Written by Nat's loving, heartbroken mom, with hopes that someday the stigma of drug addiction and loving someone with a drug addiction will no longer exist.

"NEGATIVE INFLUENCES OF A POSITIVE MAN V2.0"

"Adam" 11/18/82 ~ 01/16/2005

"NEGATIVE INFLUENCES OF A POSITIVE MAN V2.0"

It has been said that talking about the death of a loved one can tear a family apart. Out of respect and love for our family, my brother, Adam's, story has not been told in such detail in 17 years almost to the exact date. This contribution is partially for me, to potentially help anyone reading this, to help someone to recognize signs in another who struggles with addiction, and to keep his story with us.

An overlapping adult life with my brother, Adam, is almost non-existent. He lost the war when I was 18 years old, which has left me to live half of my life, now, without him. He was only 22 years old. Truth be told, this contribution will mostly be focused on his addiction and downfall, in reasonable chronological order, while sparing the details of our brotherly arguments/disagreements, and our early childhoods. This is not to neglect the person he was and came to be during his adult life. The memories that have since faded are retrievable via a fantastic decision on my behalf, to write an 8-page college essay just months after his passing. I've read it a dozen times over the years and allowed certain people in our lives to read it as well. It tells about the person he was, and keeps his positive memories and personality alive.

THE CLUBHOUSE

We were barely 8 and 12 years old when our parents decided to build us a getaway in the form of a clubhouse in the back yard. It was a child's dream. On 7-foot-tall pillars, this was a castle in my 8-year-old eyes! Insulated walls, a carpeted floor, bunk beds with mattresses, windows, a locking door, and our father had even run electricity and cable 50 yards away for it. We had a tv, video games, and heat. My brother and I spent many great sober nights together, and with our friends, playing games in the clubhouse for a few years after its construction. What began as an amazing idea turned later into a party shack for Adam and his friends. It started with pot and alcohol. He began having everyone come over to sign the drywall in the clubhouse. There are also quotes on the walls from the times they've had. I remember being so upset with him for disrespecting what took my father so much time and energy to build, and what had been paid for with my parents' hard-earned money. After the writing started, there were holes in the drywall. I have gone up those stairs no more than 3 times since. The next to last time I was there, I saw writing on the wall in his handwriting that will stay with me forever. Whether it's a quote or his own words are beyond me. Either way, they aren't my words, so it gets quotes. "Love and pain are one in the same, broken hearted the truth remained. A shitty life is no fun. Open mouth, insert gun." This speaks volumes, as an adult now, as to the unimaginable mental struggles he went through at such a young age. This seclusion just 50 yards away from our home, is where I believe his alcohol and drug abuse began.

"NEGATIVE INFLUENCES OF A POSITIVE MAN V2.0"

15-21 YEARS OF AGE

In his adolescent years, my brother Adam was as carefree as imaginable. He kept a small circle of good, close friends. Some of them were mutual between us. The people he was close to and could trust got to grow up with him and see who he really was. He had no filter or shame, always stood out in a crowd, and didn't mind how much anyone judged him. He spoke his mind to the point that I didn't know whether to be embarrassed or proud. Regardless, it was admirable. These friends, along with his long-time girlfriend, were all he needed to be happy for the longest time until we could tell he began using.

His girlfriend, we'll call her K, is the one who really kept him from spinning out of control and kept his feet on the ground most of the time. The good group of friends we knew did the same, but not as K did. She was his motivation until his final days and visited a few times even years later. K became like a sister to me, spending every moment at our home for almost 6 years. She and our parents had become very close and they took her in as one of their own. They experienced many firsts together, including his emotional rollercoaster of drug abuse.

There was only one instance that, while staying up late as teenagers do, he asked me to smoke pot with him. From stories I've heard, this one being no exception, for a true addict, marijuana really is the gateway drug. For most, it's the chance to begin mellow and test the waters. What does the high feel like from other drugs? Why am I not getting the same feeling I once did? Will less of something else be better than more of another? It escalates so quickly, that in most cases, the family and friends have no idea how bad it is until it's too late.

His poor judgement under the influence led him to attempt to ride my father's motorcycle through the yard late one night, and lay it down. It was left in the middle of the yard until the next day. I was confronted the following day and was originally the one being questioned. Neither ever mentioned a confession, conversation, redirection of fault or the topic again, and it was dropped as if it never happened. I was 16 years old and felt no need to point the finger. This was also just before my naïve, 16-year-old, still reasonably innocent-to-substance mind, understood the severity of why it had happened.

This is also around the time of another shareable instance that occurred during the late summer to early fall of 2004. At this point, our family knew he had been using for a short time. Our parents confronted him about it and had many discussions that they had kept away from me. Our bedrooms were on the same floor of the house and side by side. I came home one morning around 1am from town to see that my brother was not sober. He was barely able to hold a conversation with me and it may have been the worst I'd ever seen him. Before going to sleep that night, I asked if he was okay and tried to talk to him. He said yes, and I felt that pushing the issue would upset him. Though concerned, I laid down to sleep, not wanting to destroy the sober relationship we had together. It was a brief sleep, as I was awakened at nearly 3:30am and went to investigate. I went out into the living room to find him on the floor. He had fallen, knocked something over, and was trying to get up by using the wall. I helped him up, set him in the recliner, and tried talking to him. He was only clothed in a pair of boxers, exposing himself, had pink lips and his hair was a mess. His response was an incoherent mumble, his eyes were rolled back into his head and twitching. I was less than 17 years old and he was 21. I quickly made him "decent" again before sprinting upstairs to awaken our parents. Later, after putting Adam to bed, our parents and I sat up for nearly an hour as I said very little, but listened to their version of tough love, and a potential solution. This is when they made the decision to discuss rehab with him the following day. My parents went upstairs, and I vividly remember laying back down in my bed to cry myself to sleep that night.

MAPLE MANOR REHAB

Just a short time before his passing, Adam attended Maple Manor rehabilitation center in Port Allegany, in the fall of 2004. For two months, my parents and I traveled together every weekend to visit. This was the longest we had spoken to him while he was clean since the beginning. It was also the longest I'd ever spent with him as an adult to understand the person he was without being high. He was active in the facility and had a new outlook on life. He was more positive with every visit, and was excited to start over. He stayed clean for some time after being released, and stayed there as happily as he could, given the distance, and his eagerness to return home. It was a nice facility and he was taking care of himself. He brought home two books that are still in the same room at my parents' house to this day. As is the story of many, the sobriety did not last long after returning home (5 to 6 months) and he began spending time with the group of people he kept distant and secret from the family.

THE NIGHT BEFORE

On January 15th, 2005, the night before his passing, I was at the home of my now ex-girlfriend. It was later in the evening, maybe 11pm, and the two of us and her parents were watching a movie in their living room. There was a knock on the door. Her mother answered it, came back around the corner looking at me, and said, "it's for you." Confused, I went to the door. It was Adam, and I stepped outside on the porch to talk to him to make sure he was okay. He did not drive at the time (maybe for the best), and had walked there. We had a brief conversation during which time I could tell he was not clean. I could tell by just looking in his eyes. He asked me how I was, we chatted, and I asked him what he really needed. He said he was hanging out with some friends in town, where he was staying for the night, but he didn't have any money. He asked if he could borrow a few dollars to get food and a pack of cigarettes at Sheetz. I asked where he was hanging out that night and who he was with, but received no answer. I asked him three times during our short conversation to just let me take him home and that we could leave right then but he said no, and that he was okay. He had opened his wallet to show me $1. I asked him directly if he really did need cigarettes. He never looked away from my eyes, smiling, and said yes, he really did. He showed me the plastic cigarette case he always carried and opened it. It had one cigarette inside. I handed him $25-the only cash I had on me at the time. We talked for maybe 2 more minutes before he said thank you, shook my hand, and started walking because it was cold. I had not felt comfortable bringing him inside after seeing his eyes and hearing him talk. As he started to walk away from the bottom of the steps, he stopped, turned around 180 degrees, looked me in the eyes again, smiled, and said the last words he would ever say to me: "I'm lucky to have such a cool brother". He left, I went inside, and went home just an hour later to sleep at my parents' house.

THE DAY OF

The following day, later in the morning, I was awakened by my father turning on the light and saying, "Adam's dead." He waited for me to open my eyes but did not wait for me to react. He walked away from the door with tears in his eyes. I ran to the door to see a police officer backing out of the driveway, and my inconsolable mother crying like I have never seen, and hope never to see again. It's an indescribable feeling to have watched others fight for whom they love, and lose the war. Everything we had to offer was not enough to beat an addiction. This is the only time I can remember ever having seen either of my parents cry, other than at my wedding day many years later. Very opposite reasons. My wife and I would have to marry each other another million times to balance the happy wedding cries with the tears over the loss of their son.

Everything around me moved so slowly, but my mind raced. As time stood still, my grandparents arrived. My father had called and asked them both to come to the house. They showed up not knowing why. I had to hear him say it again. My grandparents also froze. They stayed and sat for some time. The rest of the day was a blur. Then the blurry day turned in to two, and so on. Before long, I was 1 of 6 pall-bearers carrying his casket down a hill in the snow.

The only thought that remained for the next 9 years was that I had handed him the $25 that killed him. Days after, when the possessions on his person were returned to our parents, I saw the cigarette case he had shown me. My parents had never heard this story, but I picked it up and opened it. It felt like he had torn the beating heart from my chest. To an 18-year-old, he might as well have. There was no way he had told me the truth that night because there was 1 hand-rolled cigarette inside. He had never bought cigarettes. I have never met the owners of the home where he was found the day he passed. All I got later were their names and the location. I also have never been told the drug that killed him, though I know who does know.

Again, I've kept emotionally distant on the subject due to the respect I have for our family. A few people have told me details they have heard, and who told them, such as where and how he was found, and the drugs revealed from the autopsy. Until such time as the ceiling of dark clouds is lifted, these will all be speculative. Which leads to…

THE POINT

To anyone still reading this, a few, final thoughts must be said. First, anyone who recommends that a family stays silent about the death of a loved one may choose to view it as saving the family, but is the resentment caused by the emotional neglect of those you love truly a better alternative? Support and listen to one another. Be a shoulder to cry on even if you have no words to speak. Answer the tough questions. Keep their memories alive and fresh.

The stigma we all hear about so often does need to be addressed here from our point of view. My brother and I shared a wonderful childhood. Looking back now, our parents kept a great balance between giving us wants and luxuries to spoil us as children, and saying "no," to instill in us the value of the hard-earned dollar, and strong work ethic. We were a close and loving family of 4 who honestly had everything we needed. Our parents raised us right and I would change nothing from that era. Maybe our location in a semi-secluded town influenced him, even after rehab, to spend time with the same wrong people. Regardless of the details in every unique story, one truth remains the same: addiction does not discriminate. It does not single out the lower-class individuals nor the wealthy.

A close relative once told me that it took her many years after the loss of my brother and her losing a husband, to believe that she was not a good friend or listening ear, and that she was not there for the family when we needed her most. To her, and to everyone: you need not live with the guilt. Forgive yourself. Our family was all of those things to Adam, and it took until 9 years after his death for me, personally, to come to terms with the fact that there is no reason to blame myself. Just love one another as strongly as you can. Do the little petty things with and for one another that seem meaningless when they happen. Be there for each other and live your lives without regret, resentment, judgment or blame. Tomorrow is never promised. JUST LOVE.

"Sometimes it seems like just yesterday. Other days it seems like a lifetime ago."

"NEGATIVE INFLUENCES OF A POSITIVE MAN V2.0"

My brother Adam nor our memories together will ever be forgotten.

Paul and Adam

RIPPLES: STORIES OF ADDICTION

Adam

"STRENGTH IS WHAT WE GAIN FROM THE MADNESS WE SURVIVE"

My story stems from a long line of alcoholics, drugs, and abuse. My mother was an alcoholic, and she was raised by alcoholics, my grandparents.

When my brother and I were around 4 and 6, our mother met a new boyfriend.

My brother and I were 5 and 7 when our father left to get a pack of cigarettes and disappeared off the face of the earth until we were adults.

My mother and her new boyfriend eventually married, and he became our stepfather. It wasn't long after that the abuse started. For the next 10 – 12 years, we would lay in bed many nights and listen to our mother get beaten up, waking to see her all bruised and swollen. We lived in constant fear, afraid all the time. We were pushed, punched, and woken up

"STRENGTH IS WHAT WE GAIN FROM THE MADNESS WE SURVIVE"

from a sound sleep with a belt being smacked across our stomachs, with no explanation except his drunken-induced rage. We would wake up to bags of garbage being dumped on us, with the stench of rotten food covering our bodies while he stood over us, yelling something that neither one of us could understand. The list goes on and on, but you get the idea of the torment we had to endure all during our childhood, all in the name of alcohol and drugs. Our pets often received the brunt of the anger, and they would be beaten, and a few of them were actually killed.

This was our life, this was our house, not a home, just a house we lived in. Our house was known as the drug house in town. People were in and out, all hours of the day. Police showed up occasionally, and our house was robbed a lot. As children, we would wake up from a sound sleep to find someone breaking into our house to steal drugs. You can only imagine how we felt as children to see strange people or sometimes our parents' friends ransacking the house in search of drugs, as we tried to lay quietly and pretend we didn't know.

Jason, my brother, and I were left with two babysitters on several occasions who made us watch porn, and then they would have us use play-doh to create "private body parts" to show to our parents! Unfortunately, both of these babysitters have committed suicide.

When we were about 10 years old, my brother and I would sneak into each other's rooms at night and cry as we would hear him beat our mother. We would talk about different ways we could possibly kill him and not get in trouble, and we would come up with different plans. It was our way of dealing with the helpless situation we were in, and it was our way of helping ourselves get through another night of our mother crying for him to stop, as he continued to beat her.

When we were 13-14 years old, our mother and stepfather gave us alcohol and drugs at home, so we could party and have "fun". Nothing at home was fun. Nothing in the house we called our home was fun. My stepfather held me at gunpoint for 3 hours because he caught me calling 911 while he was beating my mom again.

We were not the only children who were abused at our house. There were also some of our friends who were victims of abuse.

I was thrown out of the house at the age of 17. Everything I had was destroyed and thrown outside, simply because I didn't put the clothes in the dryer.

My mother fell heavily into alcoholism and had started to binge on drugs off and on throughout the years. I would beg her to get help over and over, but my plea fell on deaf ears. My mom worked as a housekeeper at the hospital, and she was in trouble a lot for smelling like alcohol. She often wore long sleeves to work so that people couldn't see her needle marks. When she would get out of work at 3 o'clock, she would head straight to the bar, where she sat till evening. She couldn't even walk or talk straight by the time she would leave there at night. When she would get home, she would call me, drunk and crying most of the time. It was a nightmare for me, and I dreaded the call. She would be tripping on acid LSD if she wasn't drunk. I cannot tell you how often she fell and broke bones because she was tripping on acid, or drunk.

My mom's best friend died from cancer in 2005. Her dying wish was for my mother to leave her abusive husband and get help. Six months later, my mother did just that! She called CAPSEA (Citizens Against Physical, Sexual, and Emotional Abuse), who were amazing. They helped her get out of the house and get her own place. We were all so hopeful that this was the turning point for her. And for a while, she was good. But, eventually, she fell back into her old habits and started getting wasted again. A neighbor used to call me and tell me that she often would see her crawl from her car and into her apartment and would be mumbling, "help me."

My mom's body was in pretty bad shape from the years of abuse, but things worsened. She was diagnosed with Oral cancer in 2010 on top of all the other things. She started taking 60+ oxycodone pills daily and drinking vodka, sometimes starting at 6am. She was constantly in the emergency room trying to get refills. Her cancer was eating away at the floor of her mouth, and she couldn't eat anything at all. She was in and out of the hospital for pancreatitis and pain, until she finally was able to have her surgery.

On January 20, 2011, my mom had her surgery in Pittsburgh. It took them 23 hours to reconstruct the floor of her mouth and to remove part of her jaw. The doctors were confident they got all cancer, and she was cancer free! Unfortunately, her body was so badly damaged from her addiction that she did not recover, and she passed away in Pittsburgh on March 14, 2011. She died from cirrhosis and heart problems. She beat cancer, but the drugs and alcohol won in the long run, and took her life.

Then, my brother, Jason, started drinking pretty heavily in his mid-20s. One thing led to another, and he started to occasionally use hard drugs, mostly heroin. He found an apartment in St Marys when he was about 25, and moved there. He did well for quite a while, just with his normal drinking.

I will never forget when I heard that he was shooting up. My heart broke. I thought he learned from watching the hell our mother went through. Why would he want to put himself through the same torment? He got worse and worse, and his eyes showed signs of the drugs. He was angry a lot and a terrible employee. He lost his job because he missed so much work to get high.

One evening he called me at 11:30pm and said, "There is a guy on my floor. I think he is dead." Yes, he sure was dead!

They had shot –up. Jason said he went into the kitchen for a drink and the guy was dead on his floor when he came out. The worst part is that he was so worried about getting in trouble for the drugs that he wouldn't even call an Ambulance. Well, I did!

Soon after that, he literally hit rock bottom. Jason lost everything; his job, his house. He had no money and needed drugs, and he was so sick. So, he decided he would walk down center street in Johnsonburg to the local pharmacy store and kick the doors in. After that, he just sat there on the curb and waited for the police to come and arrest him. He wanted help, he just didn't know how to ask for it.

The arresting officer said that was one of the saddest things he had seen. The officer arrested Jason, and he went to jail. He got to go to counseling and rehab. But as soon as he could, he was right back to using heroin, and now, he had found fentanyl.

When our mom was so sick with cancer, Jason never helped out because he only cared about himself and getting high. I now understand that is how addiction is. I did everything for her. I was the one that took care of her. When she passed away, I think it really bothered him, and he was consumed with guilt that he never spent any time with her while she was in the hospital. She had life insurance, which we used for her funeral and burial. What was left, we spilt. What Jason had left went to drugs.

Jason spent his 37th birthday in hospital in September, 2011. He had taken so much that he couldn't walk or move around. He was like that for three days. That was only a short time after our mother had passed. He still didn't learn, and went right back to using.

Jason and I both worked in the same plant in St Marys. Our Human resource person called me and said that Jason didn't show up for work, and he never called off. They went on to say that Jason wasn't answering anyone's phone call. I asked my husband to please go check on him because I was in the shower when they called. When my husband got there, he wasn't able to open the door. We had to call the police and they had to break the door to get in. There he was, lying on the floor with a needle still in his arm. He had been gone for hours. He had overdosed on fentanyl. Eight months after our mother died, I lost my brother, also, to this horrible demon! When we got the autopsy back, a cocktail of other drugs was found in his system. Fentanyl was the final straw, but it wasn't the only drug.

Anyone who knew Jason knew he was a good, sweet, kind person. He would never hurt anyone or anything, and he never stole from anyone to support his habit! The three of us; my mother, my brother, and I, all suffered from depression and anxiety from living in fear and being scared for our whole lives. We had to fight for our lives, fight back against the abuse we were subjected to. It wears a person down. We were just children, and we were stuck in a living hell.

I was the only one who sought medical treatment and help from the damage done to us. I knew I wanted a better life, and I didn't want to be a victim my whole life. He had taken enough from me. I wasn't giving him any more power over my life.

My family is gone, lost to alcoholism and drugs, but at the root of it all was the abuse that we lived with every day.

If you are in a situation with children, think about them and get help, leave, and run as fast as possible. You don't have to live that life!

If you are in active addiction, no matter what it is, there is help and hope. So, don't give in. You can do it.

~In loving memory of my mother and brother.
Always in my heart.~

Brandy Warmbrodt Miller

"ADDICTION IS NOT A CHARACTER FLAW"

"Steven Lee Gnan" 12/13/1979 ~ 4/30/2021

"ADDICTION IS NOT A CHARACTER FLAW"

Steven Lee Gnan Jr. was my first-born child. His arrival on December 13, 1979, was only eight days after my 18th birthday. My labor was fast and easy. In fact, it was so fast that his precious little head was crowning when the doctor arrived in the birthing room. Steven was definitely in a hurry to join this world. He lived his life the same way, always in a hurry. He was joined by his sister 17 months later. They had a great early childhood, chock full of fun and love. During their early teenage years, I'm embarrassed to admit, I became entangled in heroin use, which started as having a hard time emotionally.

At first, I just thought I could just use a little lift. I liked how the drug made me feel uplifted, energetic, and outgoing. At first, it was all fun and games, BUT it quickly makes your body need more and more of the drug to achieve the same high. It robs you of caring for anything except when your next high will be. Before long, your body craves more and more. Even after using more of the drug, you start to feel only semi-normal, with no high at all. Without the drug, your entire body, mind, and even soul, cries out in excruciating pain. Your head and heart know that you need to stop, but your body says otherwise, and a terrible cycle occurs. You're sick and tired of being sick and tired. Every time you fight to get clean, your body succumbs to the pain. This is the stage, "in my humble opinion," when drug addicts use too much, and overdose becomes more prevalent. For me, this cycle went on for a few years. My poor children were going through a living hell. They wondered if they would find me dead in the morning, or they would think they were the only white trash teenagers with an addicted parent, who cared more about the drugs than them. Only by the grace of God did I finally hit my rock bottom and find the courage to go to rehab, to try to live a normal life. I relapsed a few times. However, in the end, I've become stronger than ever.

I don't know if I believe in a predisposition to addiction or not. I do know drug addiction is a disease and should be treated as such. Both of my children became addicted to drugs. My daughter Jessica became addicted to pain pills given for a long-term injury. She accepted our family intervention and went to rehabilitation. I am proud to say she is a thriving member of society. Living her best life today.

My son, Steven, rejected our many attempts to get him to go to rehab. We tried every trick we knew, even attempting to get him incarcerated. Sadly, Steven lost his battle that dreadful day. Steven was walking on the railroad tracks behind his home. He did this daily because it was a shortcut to the local convenience store. However, he was so close to an overdose he never saw, felt, or heard the blaring and constant horn blowing as the train rounded the curve. According to investigators, my son was oblivious to the impending impact! The coroner told me that "my son was walking dead" His toxicology results were through the roof, and he died upon impact. Those details and the "would've, should've" won't bring him back to us. My hope from

"ADDICTION IS NOT A CHARACTER FLAW"

exposing our drug addictions is to plant one seed that will help others learn from it. It is worth the embarrassment.

I want to make a few points. These are just things I feel are important to share from our experience.

1.) The stigma surrounding addiction, for me, feels like a family from years ago, locking a child away due to being labeled "mentally challenged" or having to wear a red scarlet A on my chest. You are considered a dirty, shameful person to be shunned by your community.

Addiction is not a character flaw. It's not something we aspire to. Addiction is a disease like any other and should be treated as one. Real, everyday people, both rich and poor, wise and simple, can become afflicted. Addiction can be treated with awareness, therapy, medication, and compassion. Most addicts have a dual diagnosis, such as depression, anxiety, and other mental illness. Often, they already feel inadequate, shameful, and a disgrace. I know I did. What's needed is encouragement and support, not condemnation, criticism, or judgment.

2.) I got to spend a few short days with Steven on his last try at getting clean, the month before his death. He tried to explain to me how much more potent the heroin was now, compared to when I used it. He said it was amplified by the addictive fentanyl, making it much more addictive. My son and I spent the day on a road trip, and I thought I had him convinced to go to rehab in the morning. I kissed and hugged him goodnight. He slipped out in the middle of the night, and that was the last time I saw my beautiful son alive!

3.) Both of my children vividly remember my making them answer the door, making excuses about why a bill wasn't paid for shut-off services, or having to explain to friends and family why I spent my days in my room, not to be bothered. Jessica completely rebelled at that time. She stayed out for days, getting into all her teenage troubles. Steven left home to live with my parents or friends. He stuffed all that trauma I caused, and distanced himself from me until I finally went to rehab.

Steven had a heart of gold. He was fiercely protective of his family and friends. Unfortunately, his life was cut short on April 30, 2021. Like so many others in our community, his addiction contributed to his death, both senseless and preventable. Writing this story was both painful and therapeutic, but it is a story that others need to hear. Stories like the ones in this book are needed to finally bring conversations about drug addiction to the forefront.

Steven Lee Gnan Jr. you will always be loved and never forgotten.

Written by Steven's Mom, Deb Gnan

PART II

RECOVERY IS POSSIBLE

RECOVERY

This next section consists of stories shared by people who have taken the leap to make a difference in this crazy world of addiction. They will make you cry, shake your head, open your heart, and make you realize that many of us are just lucky.

These people have opened up a very private part of their life and their journey in hopes of helping you, the reader, to better understand what is it like to be in their shoes, in their mind, and in their world.

I hope you are able to recognize how hard it was for them to open up and share this with us. It is only through this recognition that we will be able to start to understand. It is only through understanding that we can begin to break the stigma.

RECOVERY

I ask you to respect each one of these brave souls who have opened up and bared their soul for you, for your children, for your grandchildren, and for the world to understand.

I also ask for you to please continue to pray for them, as this battle isn't ever over for them. Addiction is a life sentence, and they will all continue to need our love, our support, and our grace.

As I always say, we can only learn from those who have walked the journey and have traveled this road. It is the only way we will be able to find the answers. It isn't in some text book but it is from their raw truth. We need to ask them because they hold the answers.

As always, I must say, "We are our brother's keeper."

"BILLY AND HARLEY"

LOVE YOU BRO

H i, my name is Harley. Many of you know me as a drug addict. I want to share my story in case I'm not here to share it one day. My story is for the broken-hearted, the lost souls, the ones who lost their fight, and the babies born into addiction. I am currently 24, but my story begins when I was 17. My father loved me, don't get me wrong, but I came from a childhood of trauma. My father was prescribed Percocet, OxyContin, Valium; doctor prescribed drugs, for pain from an injury. This was how my own drug use started. My father was my personal drug dealer. He would hand out oxys for my friends and I to smoke.

My friends and I experimented with acid, ecstasy, coke, and shrooms in-between the oxy. Eventually, my father was cut off from his pills, so opiates became the new high, but those also became obsolete. So, what was there left to do? My best friend, my love, heroin. I wasn't bad yet, and my brother helped me get cleaned up with suboxone.

Now I'm going to fast forward to my brother's death. I won't mention names because I wish to keep her identity anonymous, but we're going to call her "D." She was there for my brother's death. Still, I dragged her into my heroin relapse. The next five years of our lives were nothing but heroin, morning, day, and night. We have spent nights crying together, wishing the sickness would end, robbing friends just to feel normal for 4 hours. We were in and out of jails. We had our ups and downs, good days and bad days.

During our active heroin addiction, we were introduced to methamphetamines, which became our second drug of choice. Of course, heroin was far more important to me than gold! Mostly the meth use was just when I was bored, or a hang-out drug. D was finally pulled out of my life by probation which hurt me badly and made me feel lost in this world. It also left me to my own demise. She was the love of my life.

So, in total, I've needed Narcan three different times... I've been in and out of jails and institutions for the last year. I've been to rehab three times. At the very first rehab, I was finally broken down enough by my addiction that I wanted to go. However, my first rehab experience wasn't a good one. I went to Pyramid in Altoona, and hated I it there. So, I walked out and gave up. During my adventure in Altoona, I ended up at an ice cream shop, where I met a man and his son. He saw me with my duffel bag and asked if I was okay. I explained the situation to him, and he said to get into his truck. On our way to the Greyhound bus station, I found out he was ten years into recovery.

The craziest part was that his son's name was Oryan. I lost a nephew by that name, so this was a big knock on the head for me. I don't believe in God, but I do believe in spirits, so I know this was a sign for me to get clean. Unfortunately, I ran into some addicts at the bus station and smoked meth the day I got out of rehab. I went home and tried to be sober but I couldn't stay sober. By this time, I was battling my addiction on my own, so I wasn't in a reasonable frame of mind. For a long time, I was trying to overdose intentionally. I finally decided that I needed to complete a program, so I went to White Deer Run, and their program was excellent. I loved it. I did my 30 days, came home, and got the Vivitrol shot. However, I didn't exactly try to make it work. I instantly went back to getting high. Now, I will cut into the story before I discuss my third rehab stay. I went as far as moving out of my county to sober up, but of course, drugs are everywhere. I kept having trouble getting clean, then I would relapse. So, I saddled up, and I went to Cove Forge, which was a decent place to be. I don't have anything bad to say about their program, but I got out and came back home to Elk County. Now, do rehabs work?

Yes, probably, for some. What it did for me was add clarity, and I've accepted that God might have a plan for me. No matter how many times I have tried to die, I have been saved. Thankfully, I have never been alone during an overdose. On April 11, 2022, I was revived by a friend after being dead for 7 minutes. In short, I've hurt the people I love the most. I've stolen, cheated, lied, and manipulated everyone around me. My mother has seen me high, and I've witnessed the heartbreak in her eyes. This is not a feel-bad-for-me story because I have put myself in this situation, so don't think I want pity. I want everyone to know what addiction has to offer, and it's nothing but insanity and loss after loss. I don't want to wake up disoriented, surrounded by cops and ambulance personnel anymore. I don't want to be sick anymore, and I don't want to hurt anybody anymore. I can only hope I win this fight for my life. I don't wish this "lifestyle" upon anyone. I've wasted too much time, energy, money, and hours looking for my next high and begging for money. I'm tired of digging my grave with a spoon. I've missed too many family events that now I won't ever get to enjoy. This disease is a family disease. It affects relationships and friendships.

I was living with a family and was working, but I still had my demons dancing with me. I got clean for 30 days, but then I relapsed. They looked past it and let me stay because they didn't want to see me in a tent, living on the streets. They believed I could do it.

I got another 30 days clean, however, those demons didn't let me rest, they came back out to play again. The lies we tell ourselves! I thought that since I had 30 days clean again, I could "celebrate" with heroin. This was almost my last time, it almost cost me my life. I was so high that I fell out of my friend's car in Johnsonburg. They took me and dropped me off at the St Marys hospital. It took eight doses of Narcan, and a ventilator to bring me back from the overdose. You would think that would have been enough? You would think that would have scared me enough that I would learn my lesson? NO, it didn't scare me, instead, it was the beginning of a three-week relapse. I lost my job, I spent all my money, and now I was homeless, broke and broken!

My best friend put me up until I went back into rehab. I spent 34 days in rehab, and then was accepted at a partial halfway house. I am on the Vivitrol shot and it hasn't been easy, but I am making it - one day at a time.

"BILLY AND HARLEY"

I am grateful for today and hopeful for tomorrow.

I hope you all forgive me one day, and I hope that I can make you all proud. I will keep fighting the good fight as I wish all my friends in active addiction will do as well. I'm still battling my addiction. I really do want to be clean! I'm fed up with getting high. RIP to the ones closest to us that we've lost. 4-14-2017 - RIP, Billy. I love and miss you. You are lost but never forgotten. Lastly, to a very good friend (you know who you are), if you are reading this, I'm sorry I put you through this battle. I hope you stay sober...

I pray my story fills someone's heart. We are people who are just lost and need to find our way again. I hope we all win this fight for our lives... Lastly, to my mother, I'm sorry, and I love you with all my heart. Sincerely, a fighting recovering addict....

I would like to close with this for all of us who still suffer:

"The Serenity Prayer"

God, grant me the serenity to accept the things I cannot change,
the courage to change the things I can,
and the wisdom to know the difference

~ Amen~

On a personal note:

I just recently lost another good friend. She lost her fight after a simple relapse. Please, if you are in recovery and you relapse, reach out before you are called home. If you are still in active addiction, please reach out for help. Your family is home waiting for the person they knew before the drug use, and they love you....

"THE STIGMA OF ADDICTION"

My name is Sarah. I am a grateful and recovering alcoholic and drug addict. I am human, just as you are. I have dreams, hopes, and goals. I did not grow up dreaming or hoping that I would have the disease of alcoholism and drug addiction. I did not grow up dreaming or hoping that I would be begging for food, stealing, or compromising my morals and values for drugs and alcohol. I am so much more than a recovering alcoholic and drug addict. I have a personality; I am important to others; and I have many purposes in life, but I believe one of those purposes is to share my experience, strength, and hope, as a way to help others.

I will begin by telling the story of what happened to me. I am 24 years old, and I was born and raised in a small town. I had an awesome childhood. My family was, and still is, filled with love and support. We would go on family vacations, have a family game and movie nights, and Sunday dinners. As a family, we ate dinner every night together. We had such unity within my family, with my parents involved in everything while we were growing up. My mom stayed home with us, and my dad worked to provide for our family. They helped us with homework and school projects, and were supportive of all of our interests.

I played softball in elementary and middle school, and my parents attended and supported me at every game. Unfortunately, I quit softball before high school because I didn't like the game's seriousness; I just wanted to play to have fun. Plus, I never really felt like I fit in anyways. In my mind, I thought I wasn't good enough or I thought I was way above everyone else; there was no in between. Looking back, I engaged in so many little behaviors that would scream to me now, saying that I had addictive tendencies, even at a young age.

My first sneaky behavior came at just eight years old when I smoked my first cigarette. I remember going home and hurrying to the bathroom to brush my teeth and shower so that my parents wouldn't know.

Alcohol always had me curious. I would see adults and teenagers drinking, and I thought, "wow, they all seem so happy and normal." I was offered sips of alcohol just to try it. I started to see that alcohol wasn't always a good time because it caused fights. It caused people to act weird too, but that didn't stop my curiosity.

Around the age of 12-13, my behaviors started to escalate. I began smoking weed, stealing alcohol, trying to find pain medication, using self-harm as a way to cope, and wanting male attention. I would lie; say I was staying at a friend's house, but went running around because their parents weren't home, or their parents thought we were sleeping. The sneaky, manipulative behaviors started to give me a feeling of normalcy. I felt less anxious and didn't feel so lonely. At times, I felt like I was on top of the world.

Those feelings ended rather quickly when I got caught. The guidance counselor at school suggested that I take drug and alcohol classes and mental health classes. Additionally, I got caught by my parents a couple of times in between. At one point, my parents grounded me and took my phone away for almost an entire year. I couldn't handle being isolated with my thoughts, so I projected them elsewhere. I snuck online, pretending to play on the computer, but I was messaging people through a text app. In addition to all of this, my best friend stopped hanging out with me: she told me I was a bad influence. Losing this friendship hurt and caused me to become more depressed.

Somewhere in between all of this, I settled down for a couple of years. I had a couple of very good friends (that I still have today.) I eventually started dating a guy on and off throughout high

"THE STIGMA OF ADDICTION"

school. The relationship was very toxic from both ends. We controlled each other, lied, manipulated, and cheated. Towards the end of our relationship, I began sneaking out, drinking, and smoking weed again. Our relationship eventually ended.

At the beginning of my senior year, I started experimenting with pain medication. I was hanging with a different crowd at this time, while keeping my other friends around when they were useful to me. I started cyber school, and began a part-time job. I wasn't physically dependent on pain pills at this point, and didn't even know it was a possibility that I could be until a friend told me. I experimented with pain pills for about four months. Once again, I wasn't anxious anymore and felt like a "normal" person. I started using my entire paycheck to buy pain pills. This is when my mom started to question what I was doing with my money because I had no bills.

June came, and I couldn't find anyone from whom I could get pain pills. I knew I would become sick if I did not find some. Finally, someone I knew informed me that there was something a little different I could buy, something I probably did not want. I was desperate and low on money, so I agreed and bought heroin for the first time. I can remember the feeling very vividly. It hit very quickly compared to the painkillers. I got a huge rush to my head, and became dizzy and warm at the same time. At this point I knew I had found what I was always searching for. At that moment, I suddenly felt peaceful and like everything was okay. Nothing else mattered.

It was from this point on that my life began to fall to pieces quickly. I remember times when my dad would allow me to use his car and I would bring it back on "E," and he would run out of gas on his way to work. I was not able to fill it with gas because all of my money went to drugs. My parents questioned me often. They knew something was not right, but I always denied everything. I was so delusional, I honestly believed that it wasn't noticeable to anyone around me. I did not think I was hurting anyone but myself. I actually didn't even think I was even hurting myself. My parents eventually found out, and I could no longer deny this problem I was facing. They helped me get into counseling and were very supportive. They tried their best to understand what was going on, but I couldn't even understand it myself.

I stopped using heroin and became extremely sick. Despite being sick, I was still going to work and trying to get my life back. After about a week of being clean, I picked alcohol back up and started drinking heavily. I was staying out all night drinking and going into work the following day, still drunk or hungover.

Somewhere along the way, I started smoking weed again too. This lasted only for about a month and a half. Before I knew it, I was back to using heroin. I also started experimenting with other drugs such as meth. I remember once, on my brother's birthday, I spent all day doing meth and had to go to a birthday dinner with my family that evening. I thought I looked and acted fine (another delusion I had.) My parents confronted me after dinner when we got home and told me I was no longer allowed to borrow their cars because they didn't want me driving under the influence. I ended up leaving that night anyway, and I had a friend come get me.

My grandfather passed away during this time and I wasn't home with my family. My mom and dad were texting me to come home and be with the family because he had passed, and we needed to be there to support each other. I didn't bother to go home. I don't even remember when I made it home, but I know that I went to the funeral. I felt nothing, I was so numb to everything at this point. I remember my mom telling me this is when she really knew I was no longer the Sarah she once knew because the Sarah she knew was the Sarah who put family first. The Sarah she knew would have never ever left family behind in a time of need. I was gone, just a shell of a person, surviving, nothing more.

I was gone for days at a time with minimal contact with my parents. They didn't know if I was dead or alive until I randomly showed up at home to get a shower, clothes, or whatever I needed. I went home one night, and the door was locked. I couldn't get in. I was so angry, I left and didn't go back home. I left all of my belongings and moved in with a guy I had met a week prior. This is where my addiction had taken a whole different turn. I began having a very steady flow of drugs and so much more than I had before. I quit my job about a week or so later because I couldn't wake up in time or just didn't feel like going. I couldn't have anyone holding me accountable because nothing mattered. The only thing that mattered was getting high. I would make trips to the city to get drugs cheaper because I couldn't pay for my habit.

I remember feeling very depressed that I couldn't be with my family. I wanted to go home so badly, but I couldn't get clean and sober and knew that it wouldn't be acceptable there. I texted my sister once, and my parents told me that that really upset her, and I couldn't comprehend why because I couldn't see how badly I was hurting everyone. I didn't know how they felt, and I believed they were better off without me. I would have dreams and wake up crying in panic attacks because I had abandoned them. Yet, I didn't want to live this life but didn't know how to stop. It was a cycle I couldn't break or even comprehend.

I tried going to rehab for the first time when I was nineteen. I could not take the pain anymore and did not know what else to do. I thought rehab would "cure" me; help me to be able to use successfully. I also had another delusion that it would make me stop drinking and getting high for the rest of my life. I thought that somehow, I could just go detox my body and lock myself away for 30 days, and that would fix everything. It would surely bring the old Sarah back. Boy, was I in for a rude awakening? I made it four days in detox, and I did not even make it to rehab. I called my boyfriend at the time and had him come pick me up. The craziness my mind went through at the time. I knew I should stay, but the mental obsession that was still there (that I was unaware of) pulled me away. There was a war going on in my mind, body, and soul, and I couldn't comprehend the slightest bit of it.

For a brief time after leaving, things got pretty bad for me. On my way down to the city, I got arrested for the first time. It was Easter Sunday and I was supposed to go to my parents' house for dinner, but I needed to get drugs first. They found out I got arrested because the officer called them to tell them I needed to be picked up, and they refused. I remember texting my dad back to resume our conversation we had earlier, and I acted like nothing had happened. I was so resentful that they wouldn't come to pick me up. (I am grateful for that now.)

I went straight back to the city to get more drugs and stayed in a hotel that night. If that isn't the insanity of this disease, I don't know what is. A "normal" person may think, "how stupid," "I would never do that again," or, "Don't you learn?" Here is the thing, an addict's brain is physiologically different. This is especially true when it is under the influence, or has been under the influence of a mind-altering substance.

At this point, I was scrounging off whoever I could, whether it was drugs, food, a place to stay, or money. It didn't matter what it was, and it didn't matter what I had to do to get it. I was surviving. I had a few jobs for maybe a week or a few weeks at a time. I remember stealing from a cash register where I worked, thinking that no one would know it was me because other people worked there. I was so delusional that I even believed the delusions. I wore long-sleeved sweatshirts so no one would notice the track marks on my arms. It was 80 degrees, so obviously, everyone knew something was up.

People looked at me with disgust, as if I did not already feel that about myself. I was just "a junkie" choosing day in and day out to live this way. But, I was not. I was once told that I was nothing more than a junkie and didn't deserve to live. I remember losing my mind at that comment and crying for hours and hours. I even contemplated suicide. I wanted so badly to die, but I also wanted so badly to be clean and sober. I wanted to feel what "normal" people felt, I wanted to live a "normal" life but I didn't know how. I did not want to live like this; no hot water for showers, no heat, and living in filth.

I started using meth pretty heavily at this point. Mentally, that was a whole different level for me. I was awake for months with only, maybe, 20-minute naps every couple of days. I was hallucinating and losing my mind every day a little bit more. I remember that when I couldn't get more drugs, I would lock myself in my closet and cut myself.

I reflect on some of the terrible things I saw during these times. I had seen children living in horrid conditions, people overdosing and no one caring, things that I would never be okay with if drugs hadn't been involved. My relationship with my boyfriend became violent, from both ends, physically, emotionally, and mentally. I was lost. I would text my parents begging to come home because our fights were getting too bad. Then when they would decide to let me, I would just tell my mom, "never mind." I can't imagine what my mom went through, not knowing what was happening and just so badly wanting to help her hopeless daughter. My boyfriend and I eventually broke up, and I moved out.

I hopped around from house to house. I eventually found somewhere to stay with food and drugs. This is the part of my story that I hardly remember. I'm not sure what was real and what wasn't. My brain was so chemically dependent, and my body was deprived of basic human needs. I don't even know how long I was staying at this house, maybe a week, maybe longer. I remember, at first, that things seemed okay, and I was getting what I needed to survive. Then, things started to change, and if I wanted to continue to stay there and keep getting the things I needed, I had to do whatever it took.

Some may ask, "Why not go home to your family?" Unfortunately, I was far too gone to make any rational decisions. My addiction took me to dark places I never want to visit again —the pits of hell. I was demoralized. Drugs controlled my life, and I did things I had never dreamed I would ever do. I remember locking myself in the bathroom because I was convinced I was going to be killed by the man I was staying with. For the sake of clarity, I will refer to this man, fictitiously, as Bert. I remember Bert telling me he was going to kill me. Maybe he wanted me to leave his house, and I wouldn't go because I had nowhere else to go where I could continue to feed my addiction. I was looking out the bathroom window and just kept seeing shadows outside. They were the people who were conspiring to kill me. Was it real? I still don't know. Although, at the time, I sure believed it was.

I called the police because I was afraid for my life. The police came and got me out of that place. I had three or four knives on me, pepper spray, and syringes. One police officer made an impression on me for the rest of my life. He finally saw that I was a person. He didn't look at me with disgust or treat me as if I were below him. He gave me a bible verse and told me that I should go to detox, and he would help me get a bed that morning. I agreed. In January 2018 I went to detox for the second time.

Detox was the most mentally horrific thing I believe I have ever gone through. I was completely out of my mind. I would call my ex-boyfriend and my parents and verbally abuse them so that they would come to pick me up. They would not come to get me. I remember repeatedly calling to get them to come to pick me up because I was convinced the hospital staff was working with Bert, and they were all trying to kill me. I thought they had my wallet in the lunch cart and would stuff my dead body in there after killing me. I thought my roommate in detox knew what was happening and was in on it too. The sound that was actually coming from the TV in the next room, was Bert. I know it all sounds so crazy, but it was my reality at the time. Like I said before, some of the stuff still seems so real almost four years later.

I spent four days in detox, the longest four days of my life. While I was there I got to eat and shower and was provided resources for more help. I went to my first 12-step meeting. My counselor had me write a pros and cons list for going to rehab. That was the first time I became honest about my addiction. I'm not sure why, but I do know that the only power that could have made that happen is my higher power. So, I made the pros and cons list as honestly as possible, and with help from my counselor and my parents, I took the next step and went to rehab. It was a 28-day rehab a couple of hours away from my hometown. While in the facility, I remember participating in some things. I would pick and choose what I wanted to do and didn't really listen to the rules. I seemed to be more preoccupied with anything other than what I should have been doing. It was a beautiful rehab though; I did learn quite a bit there.

That's when I first realized there were others like me. I was not the only one who had done horrendous things for drugs. Little by little, I would let my secrets out, and I began to realize that I wasn't alone. Finally, talking to my counselor in rehab made me come to terms that I was not just addicted to drugs, I was also an alcoholic. Every time I relapsed on heroin or whatever drug, the relapse usually started with alcohol.

At the end of my stay, something inside me told me I should take it to the next step. I knew that if I went home, I would end up in the same cycle that I had always ended up in. The decision was hard because I was still obsessed with the idea of getting drunk or high. So, I tried something new and went to a halfway house that was 2 ½ hours away. I had arrived at a halfway house near Wilkes-Barre, PA. I remember the terrible feeling I felt when I arrived there. I felt so homesick and wanted to go home very badly. I cried and cried because I didn't know how to cope with things, other than running away from them. Here I was, headfirst in a very uncomfortable, unfamiliar situation without drugs and alcohol to cope.

My stay at the halfway house was four months. In those four months, I was lying, sneaking, obsessing, overthinking, and still running on fear. I wanted to get better, but I didn't know how to do it. I was only willing to take some suggestions at the time. I was stealing and taking other people's medications, and I thought it was okay because they were not narcotics. I ended up having two seizures while I was there because of how much medication I was taking. I acted like I didn't know what it was from, but I had an idea. I eventually left the halfway house and went to a sober house. I was there for about a month and ended up using heroin on and off again. I wanted to be clean and sober so badly, but I couldn't figure out how to become willing to do so. I got honest with the house manager because she knew I was getting high again. She was willing to give me another chance and not kick me out, which I am very grateful for.

Another month went by, but I didn't change. I was still doing some of the same things I was before. I was still engaging in old behaviors and thinking it was okay because I wasn't getting drunk or high. I picked alcohol back up and instantly started trying to find heroin again. So, I was back at it. Getting high again until I told my house manager about a week later. I couldn't take it anymore. I didn't understand why I kept going back to the same thing that destroyed my life. I did not have another coping mechanism. I did not know life anymore without drugs or alcohol, but at the same time I couldn't stand to have drugs or alcohol in my life. I went through a great deal of mental agony that left me feeling baffled and hopeless. Most days I wanted to die because I felt so defeated and I was out of solutions. I was honest with my house manager about what was going on, and she put me in a relapse prevention class.

I was not only honest with her, but I was finally honest with myself. I needed help because I didn't know another way. I am an alcoholic. I am a drug addict. I cannot successfully use alcohol or drugs. My brain is physically different from a "normal" person's brain. I have an allergy to alcohol and drugs, and the second I put any drug (including alcohol) in my body, I flare up, and it causes me to become mentally obsessed, and the cycle starts all over again. I will become physically dependent and spiritually drained. I will no longer be the Sarah I am or want to be. I asked my higher power (with whom I was very estranged), "help me, just help me. I cannot go on like this." That's when I finally gave up, I had surrendered. I wasn't fighting anymore, and I couldn't.

I started taking suggestions from a 12-step program. That was the only thing I had seen working for the people around me. I saw the freedom I had seen in their eyes and souls, and I wanted that. They couldn't be like me? I was different from them. I came to find out, they are exactly like me.

So that is the blessing my higher power chose for me. A 12-step program that I am forever grateful for. When I was about five months sober, I met my boyfriend, who is also in recovery. When I was six months sober, I found out I was pregnant with my son. I wanted to be a mother so badly. I didn't even know how to love myself or who I was at this point. I had just started figuring out who I was and what I wanted. I believe God blessed me with my son to give me the push that I needed. I was scared for my child's life. I did not want to go back to the old life I had been living, especially since I was bringing a child into this world. I could not live with myself if I lost him because of this disease. I knew he would not be able to keep me sober so I clung on as tight as I could to my support group of strong women. At this point, my higher power gave me the willingness I needed to finish my first set of lifelong steps that were suggested in my 12-step program. I finished them for me. After I completed the personal inventory and shared it with my sponsor; that is when my sobriety truly started. I was able to take an honest look at the damage I had caused because of the fear and resentment I had festering inside of me. I was never aware of my behavior patterns or my character defects. I knew something was wrong with the way I acted, but I was clueless as to why.

I know now that fear and resentment will be the death of me. I had to gain a stronger relationship with my higher power. None of this came all at once. It was as if I was building a relationship with a friend (my higher power) and finding my true self. They always say time takes time and I couldn't understand that. Today it makes more sense. My higher power always discloses what I need to hear at that moment.

Most days I can fully rely on my higher power and trust that whatever happens is meant to be. However, there are times when I still take my will back, get scared, or angry. The difference today is that with the help of others and my higher power, I can quickly realize when I am doing that and try to get back on track. I try not to let it fester within myself because that's when I become toxic again and I don't even realize it. I can deceive myself so easily at times. That is why it is so important for me to stay in touch with people in the program. I ended up moving back home, and my boyfriend came with me. We had our beautiful son a couple of months later and instantly fell in love with him.

At this point, I was a dry drunk (Staying sober but not working the program that I needed.) I had a million reasons not to do what I needed to be doing for my recovery. My delusions started talking to me in my head again after some time. "You can drink again," and they continued and happened more frequently. I was so fearful because to me, it proved that even when I take the alcohol and drugs away, if I am not continuing the daily treatment I need for my disease of addiction, I will not survive this, and addiction will always get the best of me. It proved to me once again that I am an alcoholic and a drug addict. My life is unmanageable, with or without alcohol and drugs, unless I keep up with my program and working the steps daily. I am the problem, not drugs and alcohol.

Drugs and alcohol are a symptom of my addiction. I used alcohol and drugs to feel "normal," and then it became a vicious cycle that I could not break on my own. I cannot do this alone, ever. I jumped back in the program, and it's been a wave of ups and downs since then, but that is life. I have been blessed with living the life I have always dreamed of.

I had the opportunity to take CRS (Certified Recovery Specialist) classes and get certified. I have been blessed with another son. I have a beautiful, healthy relationship with my boyfriend and all of my family members. My higher power has given me life and regenerated my soul. Life is beautiful and with the help of my higher power and my support system, I can get through anything that life throws at me. It may be painful at times, but nothing can compare to the pain I experienced from addiction. I never thought this was possible. I did none of this myself. My higher power and the people he used to get me here today have everything to do with my sobriety and giving me another chance at life. I have to rely on my higher power, do deep, self-searching inventories, continue to correct the past, and continue to pass along what was so freely given to me.

I am blessed with many opportunities today. I am a daughter, sister, mother, and girlfriend, and there are so many other parts to me. My journey is not over. It's a lifelong practice of daily maintenance and willingness, with the help of my higher power. I would not trade my life or any of the challenges in it for anything in the world. I do not regret my past. I am a grateful RECOVERING alcoholic drug addict.

~ Recovery is Possible ~

"FROM OUT OF THE SHADOWS SHE WALKS LIKE A DREAM"

Hi, my name is Ashley I was born in Coudersport, PA but raised in St. Marys, PA. My parents were together but got divorced when I was two years old. I am an only child. My grandparents raised me, and all of the childhood memories I have are because of them. I was okay with it, I loved being with them! My grandparents hold a very special place in my heart, and have been there for me since day one in this world.

Growing up was your normal home, boring, and always getting in trouble for something I had done. My most important memories so far are with my children and remembering all the good memories that we had with their father before he passed away this year (2022). So, life was life. I got together with my children's father back in 2010. We eventually got married in 2015. Then we had a very heartbreaking death in the family, which led to us being introduced to IR 30 pills. IR 30s are an opiate prescription used for severe pain. After months of taking them, it turned into a bigger addiction. I realized that the pills weren't doing it for me anymore and that I needed something stronger to get me higher. When I was introduced to heroin, it became my drug of choice. The first time I did it I absolutely loved it and enjoyed the high much more. I was just outside my body, numb and couldn't feel. I just was there. The only reason I numbed myself was to deal with the loss of someone close, to deal with three kids, and struggling every day. It all started to overwhelm me, and it was the only thing I could do to take the stress of life away. Eventually, after getting really badly into my addiction, I lost my children to Children and Youth. That's when I finally hit rock bottom and knew I needed help. The day right after my kids got taken, I went to jail for 30 days. I then went to Turning Point rehab for their 30-day program. It was an amazing experience. I learned a lot about my disease and how to cope with it daily. I learned positive ways to keep my sobriety going. It completely changed who I was. I was so happy, smiling, and clear-headed. I got me back! It was the best feeling ever. I only needed to go to rehab one time to realize how badly I messed everything up, not only addiction-wise but my mental health was not in a good place. I graduated from rehab on November 14th, 2020. I have been clean ever since. Working, staying sober, having my own apartment, and having such amazing support to get me through my days. You all already know who you are, and I am truly blessed to have you all! This summer I graduated from Drug& Alcohol, and Dr. Hall's program.

I have truly come so far in the last two years, I live life to the fullest, and love my children extra hard. I am still fighting for them, but they will be returning home soon! Recovery is possible, and I'm so blessed to have won the fight, and to keep on winning the fight. Recovery looks amazing on me, and I'm not scared to show it! I have hit rock bottom and lost a lot of people close to me! The most important thing I remember is that I'm waking up every day with another day sober. If you are struggling with addiction please, please do not be afraid to reach out. All of us recovering addicts are in this together, and we shall continue to fight this battle as one. We have lost too many people in this world already, it's time we start making a difference. To stay clean and sober, I do NA meetings and I meet with a counselor. Also, reading the book, *Just for Today* has helped me get to where I am today.

~ **Ashley**

"CAN WE SKIP TO THE GOOD PART?"

We all make choices in our life. Some choices are good, some are bad, and some are out of our control. Yeah, I know that might sound crazy, but when you are an addict, it feels like every choice you make isn't really YOUR choice. Addiction is a voice in your head telling you to do things that you know are wrong, and you know could get you in trouble, lose the people you love, and lose everything, but nothing else matters besides getting that next high. That voice in your head overpowers you, and before you know it, you are stealing, lying, and becoming someone you swore you would never become. Before I was an addict, I remember hearing stories of addiction and what addicts do, and I always would say, "how can someone do that?" "I would never put drugs before my children." I was so quick to judge, and little did I know a short time after, I would become one of those addicts, and over time I was living that life that I would never have ever thought I would live. I am an addict.

First things first, addiction does not discriminate. It doesn't care if you are rich or poor, black or white, the age you are, if you live in a mansion or on the streets. It can happen to anyone within the blink of an eye. I had a tough childhood. I went through some traumatic events that most kids my age don't go through until they are adults. My dad died right before I would have turned 2. I don't remember him and only have a handful of pictures. So, from then on it was my mom, my three older sisters, and me. Obviously, it was rough growing up without a dad, but my mom did the best job. My dad's parents (my grandparents) were always a big part of my life. I also had the three best big sisters anyone could ever ask for, and to this day, through my years of addiction, they still are my biggest supporters. Fortunately for my sisters, they had a different dad than I had, but since I can remember, their father never treated me any differently than his own daughters. That includes Christmas, birthdays, etc. On the weekends, I could go and spend the night there with my sisters, and he always made me feel welcomed into his home. He and my mom never made me feel left out from not having a dad. My mom was my best friend and gave me the best life she could. Unfortunately, she was diagnosed with cancer. I remember leaving school early (elementary school) to go with her to chemo and radiation. She fought so hard. My mom was put on hospice, and we moved a hospital bed into my room so that she and I could share a room.

Some of the best memories I have of her were from when she and I shared a room. She lost her battle when I was 12 years old. So, if you can remember being 12 again, imagine how confusing life is and how carefree it's supposed to be. Imagine not having your mom or dad there through that and then being uprooted from your family, friends, and the only town you ever knew days after your mom's funeral. I was sent to live with my aunt and uncle in Philadelphia.

I will keep it short here, but my aunt and uncle were wealthy. They gave me a good life. I lived at the Jersey Shore every summer, went on vacations, and had everything I could have imagined. Money isn't everything, though; it definitely does not buy happiness. Please keep in mind that addiction does not run in my family. My aunt and uncle raised me well. I knew right from wrong. I went to school every day, had a good group of friends, didn't get in trouble, and didn't even curse, LOL I lived with them in Philadelphia from the age of 12 until I graduated high school when I was 18. I saw my sisters twice, maybe three times in all those years. It was like my old life was forgotten, but there wasn't a day I didn't think about, "what if my mom and dad were here?" After I moved back home, I instantly got a job waitressing and did that for years. I was gone for so long, so I didn't really have any friends, so I worked all the time, and my other time was spent with my grandparents or my sisters. I went to college at Lock Haven University of Clearfield. I originally went to get into their nursing program, but that's not where my heart was. I took a medical assistant course, and after a few months became a CMA. Unfortunately, there weren't many jobs hiring for a CMA at that time, so I became what I thought was the next best thing a CNA. I loved it. I was able to lease my first car on my own, I had a job that I loved, and all of this by the time I was 21, so I figured I was on the right path, and my family seemed so proud of me. That was true for only a short time.

After college and working, I began to make friends, but I think I was so desperate to have friends that it led me to not a good group. As a result, I got myself into some trouble (not drug related. Yet), which ruined my best relationship with my grandparents. They did not speak to me for a couple of years. I wish then I had sought more help with all of the mental health issues I had before it led me to drugs. If I had known then what I know now.

I first got high when I was 23 years old. I fell one night, and I fractured my ankle, and got prescribed Percocet. I've been prescribed them before and always would take them as prescribed with no issues. Unfortunately, my group of friends was still not the greatest this time. At all. To this day, I still think if I had never met a select few people, would I have gotten high or become addicted? Only God knows the answer to that. Anyway, I picked up my prescription, and the friend I was with suggested that we snort the pills and that the pain would go away a lot faster by doing that. So, I figured I mean, why not? It can't hurt, and I just wanted to fit in with what my 'friends' were doing at that time.

Well, obviously, my prescription was gone in about three days, and I was hurting. Well, then I was told that I could buy pain pills. I thought I would be buying the same thing I was prescribed, but boy was I wrong. The pills I bought were called 'blues and Opanas" (a.k.a Oxycodone). One was $40.00 for one pill, and the other was $60.00 for one pill. The amount of money I've spent on drugs alone makes me sick. But all the people I hung out with were doing them, so I just didn't want to be the only one not doing it. Not only was I doing it, and buying them for myself, I was also buying them for the people that would get them for me. So like clockwork, that became my life for a few months. I would go to work, and as soon as I was done I would get picked up and go get pain pills and go back to my apartment and just get high all night, just to do it all over again the next day. There were some days when I was broke because, let's face it, being an addict is SO expensive, so when I couldn't buy anything for myself or anyone else, those were the days I would spend alone. I knew those people weren't my friends, and I was just being used, but it felt out of my control to stop being around them. The second I got paid, we would all be back together again, and I would forget how awful I felt when alone.

You know how people go to the bar and have a drink and hang out? In my friend group, we would go to someone's house and get high all night, and at that time, it seemed harmless, and we weren't bothering anyone, so what was the big deal? Well, the big deal was doing these pain pills for months, you eventually build a tolerance, so you go from needing one pill a day to 2 or 3 even to get "high," and what's the point of doing a drug if you aren't going to get high? Deep down, I knew what I was doing was wrong but it just took control so fast. I never wanted to tell anyone "no." Peer pressure and people-pleasing were my biggest flaws in life and, obviously, my addiction. Some people laugh when they talk about that, but peer pressure is very real. So, between that and just trying to be a people pleaser, I felt like if I had what people wanted, I would always have someone to hang out with and never be alone. I used to just hang out with my sisters when I was bored and had no one else, so I just don't know why I never picked up the phone to call them. I would want to, and then I would remember what I was doing, and I just always thought if they knew, they would cut me out of their life. I wish I knew that was never the case. They may get mad, upset, hurt, and angry with me, but they were always there for me, time and time again. I will forever be grateful to God for giving me the best three older sisters anyone could ever have.

Okay, so let's talk about when I was in active addiction. That lasted on and off for about 6 years. I will never forget the first night I tried heroin like it was yesterday. It was five years ago, but I can remember where I was, where I was sitting, who was there, the temperature outside, and the time of day. I could paint you a picture of that night, but that's what heroin does. It was a feeling that literally took my breath away and was like nothing I have ever experienced before. I loved it. Everything I was stressing about disappeared. I was so happy and felt like nothing could ruin my mood. Then the high wore off, and all I wanted was to feel like that again, and that's how it gets you. Heroin was also a lot cheaper than the pain pills I was doing so it just made sense at the time to pay for whatever you'd get more of. I started meeting new people that also did heroin, and that's what our nights became. As soon as the high wore off and the drugs were gone, it's like that's all that consumed you. All you can think about Is getting that next high, or if you were broke, that started the process of trying to figure out how to get money to get more. There is so much more that goes into being an 'addict' than simply doing drugs. It literally changes your whole lifestyle. The version of you that you once were before ever getting high is completely gone. You become someone not only does your family not know, but you begin not even to know yourself. You start doing so many things you never would think that you would do. There are so many people that would say, "if I had kids, I would get sober," or "you're a mom, how can you not think about your babies?" Believe me when I say becoming addicted doesn't stop or change just because you become a parent. Sometimes I felt like my addiction got worse after having kids, which I know sounds awful, but it's the truth. There were so many things I went through in life and so many issues within me that I needed to work on If I ever wanted to be sober, but I just kept telling myself I was fine, and at least when I was doing drugs, all of those issues and problems I have just don't seem anywhere near as important as getting high. I never understood why I couldn't just be alone with myself, like myself, and why I always wanted to have friends or people to like me. I never truly figured out the problem until I got sober, put the work in, and actually wanted to be sober. It is so easy for people to say, "just stop," but it isn't so easy to stop. The drugs literally take over your mind. It's sickening. Part of me wanted to get sober so many times. I knew the people in my life didn't deserve half of the things I put up with or did for them, but I also hated myself for so long, so people pleasing just became like second nature.

I was 23 when I found out that I was pregnant with my oldest son. When I got pregnant, I was only dating John for about one month, maybe two so we barely even knew each other. And that first month or two we weren't even really in a relationship, he would go back and forth between another girl and me, and then I found out I was pregnant so like most girls, I was dreaming of that perfect family. I will always blame myself for this, but when John and I first met, he didn't do drugs like I did, so I introduced him to the drugs and my friends, and he became addicted essentially because of me. When I got pregnant, I quit doing everything, but he kept getting high. I may not have been getting high, but I was still around the drugs and that lifestyle my whole pregnancy, and let me tell you, that is sometimes just as bad. Being around that same group of people, watching them get high, and knowing I couldn't just caused me to be mean and irritated. And again, that sounds shitty, but it's the truth. It would just cause fights, and rage, and lies. John would lie a lot, but the truth always comes out. So once the lies started and he chose to keep getting high, and I didn't, I should have just ended it, but as I said before, I was having a baby with him, my first a boy, and I just wanted to be a family. He was so excited to be a dad and have a son so I kept thinking that he would stop once our son was here, but that is easier said than done. There was also a lot of mental abuse during that time, some pushing and shoving, a lot of anger. I would have a phone for maybe two months, and he'd get mad and break it. I tried not to take it to heart because I knew parts of it were because he was getting high and he wasn't himself, so I kept thinking, this won't last forever, we're having a baby, we love each other. So, I thought. He was my first actual relationship and at first, I was in love. Like every relationship, there were good and bad days, but once our son was here, everything would be perfect.

Nine months went by, and our first baby was here. John was in the hospital with me for three days until I had him by my side, and I thought things would be different. It lasted probably a week, and then the drugs came back. I wasn't pregnant anymore, so I figured we could have fun one night since we didn't have the baby, and that would be it. Very funny. Every addict knows there isn't just ONE time. At that time, I didn't understand about changing your whole friend group to stay clean. I was still new to addiction, so I figured we could still hang out with the same people and not get high. Anyone who tells you that they can, is lying. I promise you. We weren't getting high every day but once a week turned into twice a week, and you know the rest. Well, a month goes by, and boom, I'm pregnant. AGAIN. I have a one-month old baby, and I got pregnant again. How does that even happen?! Well, it does. We were brand new parents and now not only had one baby to care for, but in 9 more months we would have another one. The addiction got worse.

We moved into a 2-bedroom house with our son and things were good at first. We had some really good days. Shortly after we moved, we got $4,000, and it went by so quick. As soon as you hand an addict, that amount of money, it's pretty much game over. Again, this whole addiction thing was all new to me, to both of us. We hid it from our family for a long time, well, we tried to. You may think you can fool your family, and you can for a little bit but eventually, it catches up to you, and they know. You can't sell drugs forever and not get caught. I'm not proud of many things we did, or the people we had around, but we were both just so wrapped up in that lifestyle, and once you live a certain way for so long, it's not easy to just change it overnight. We would let people stay over all the time, let people sell drugs from our house, and eventually, that led to us personally having our own dealer that would only deal with us. Then we would sell the drugs for him. It was smart for him, he made a bunch of money and only dealt with us. We took the risk of meeting people all day and night. When you sell drugs, people will do literally anything for you. Everyone wanted to be our friend and be at our house. People will do anything to get high. Our house was just a revolving door. I honestly can't even think of when it was just John, me, and our son. Someone was always there and this went on for weeks. Soon enough, word got around to the cops. I remember sitting in my bed, looking out my window and seeing the cops parked right across the street in front of our house. You would think we would stop, but no. Not only were the drugs an addiction so was the whole lifestyle and the money. Neither of us worked, so that was our income for a while. Basically, we just sold drugs to support our habit. At the time, that is all we cared about. Also, during that time, our relationship was so bad. There were so many times I wanted to stop everything and leave, but again, easier said than done. There was a lot of mental abuse and that eventually turned to physical abuse. How can you hit a person you love? I thought the same thing but the drugs were a big part of it. I know I played a role in things and didn't always help the situation, but when you are with someone and its toxic, and it gets bad, and you want to leave, you can just feel stuck. For anyone in a toxic relationship who doesn't think they can leave, I can tell you now, just leave. But at that time, I wasn't thinking clearly. He wasn't thinking clearly, either. There were a lot of factors at play. Well, one day we were told the cops knew what we were doing and we would get busted so that was a little wake-up call. However, it didn't last long. We would go for periods of a few months sober, but always found our way back. Out of all the people I thought were my friends, only ONE of them was a sober friend. We would hang out, and I think deep down she knew what was going on but never really wanted to believe it. It is easy to lie to people when you're high. No one wants to admit they are addicted to drugs. the hardest part of addiction is actually admitting that you are an addict. It took me almost four years to say it out loud.

There was a guy from Pittsburgh who would come to Elk County to sell heroin because he made a lot of money, here. He started staying at our house whenever he came to town. When he left, he would leave the drugs with us to sell and then come back for the money and more drugs. I felt like the whole town was coming to our house. That's what it felt like. Let me say, if you really knew some of the people that really do get high, you would be so shocked. I couldn't believe some of the people I met, I would never have expected half of them, but hey, addiction does not discriminate, as I said before. This went on until I had my second son.

When I had my second son, it was just me and John, which was so different from when I was in labor with my first. John was still in active addiction, so the whole time, he was either withdrawing or high, or if he wasn't high, he was mad that he didn't have drugs, so the overall experience was just not great.

Until this point, I had never tried methamphetamine. I always said, "I will never do that. It's just chemicals. I won't do that to myself." Little did I know. I actually remember coming home from the hospital with my 2nd born, and trying meth for the first time. Wow. I was home with a ten-month-old and a newborn baby. Obviously, I made a choice to have two babies that close, and I would never change that for the world, but it was A LOT. After a few hours of being home, I realized how hard it would be, and of course, someone was at our house and had meth. He said, "here try this. You won't be tired anymore." So of course, being an addict, I tried it. and as soon as I tried it, I could just feel my heart racing, and it was like I instantly got so much energy. Meth became my new favorite drug. I wasn't ever tired. I felt like I could clean the house, be awake with my boys, and be more attentive. But that was just the drugs talking. Physically I may have been there every day and night, but mentally I was so far gone. It took me forever to realize I needed to take care of myself first if I wanted to be able to take care of my children. I will always regret not being the best mom that I could have been when my boys were babies. They didn't deserve the life we gave them for the first few years of their life, and I have to live with that. I mean, I had my kids all day, every day. It was very rare if you saw me without my children. In reality, I wasn't a good mom at all. There was still a lot of fighting between me and John, and there were many people around that shouldn't have been around, and they didn't deserve that. At any time, we could have lost them, but that thought never crosses your mind. You never think it will happen to you, but let me tell you, it happens. I will get to that. John begged and begged his parents for us to move in with them, and they told us no quite a few times before they finally said yes. As far as my family is concerned, all I have are my sisters, but at this point they would hear things about us dealing drugs, and every time I would deny and deny. They also weren't fans of our relationship, and they tried many times to help me to leave, but I always went back. I will never blame them for distancing themselves from me, either. They disagreed with my choices, and I don't blame them for not wanting any part of what I got into. But if I ever called, they would always answer. I was just so embarrassed about what I was doing because I knew I was better than the person I had become. Also, disappointing your family and the people who love you is hard. So, by Halloween of 2018, we were living with John's parents, which was probably the best thing to have happened at the time.

We were sober for a little bit living there, but I will continue to say this because it is so important: If you don't change the people, places, and things, you will keep returning to your old life. We changed the place but not the people. We both started working for the first time in years, and since we were living with his parents, we could save money. That didn't last but a few months, and then I found out I was pregnant again. Now, I had a 2-year-old and a 1-year-old and I was pregnant again. I will always be thankful for his family letting us live there with our kids and helping financially when the boys needed things, but it wasn't always the best situation. There's that stress of having your own family, living with your parents, and not having your own space in a relationship. It became a lot sometimes and it seemed that whenever we got stressed, the first thing we both turned to, to cope, was going back to drugs. Even though we would have a few months clean, we would send one message to one person, and it would all be over. We were just getting back to our normal selves, or so it seemed, and then we went back to using. Then, you're back to that person you don't even know. His family definitely put up with a lot more than they should have, but with two kids and one on the way, they would never have just put us out on the street. I was due with my youngest right around Christmas. We decided to get married before he was born, so we went to the courthouse and got married the day before I had my youngest. One of my sisters went and his mother and sister and brother. I remember how upset my sister looked, so disappointed. I mean, at least she came, but just that look she had was like, "Kelsey, what are you freaking doing?" We were together for 3 years by now, and we had three boys together. So, despite all the bad things we were still a family and he was my first love. For some reason, I thought if we were married, everything would be okay. I'm not saying I didn't love him, because I think at that point I really did. Also, it was just comfortable. Even though we were completely toxic for each other, I knew him, and it felt easier to stay than have to start over with three boys. He always threatened that he'd have my kids taken if I left him, or that he'd plant drugs on me so that I'd get in trouble, or that he would tell my family I was an addict. He told me that I am gross, and I would never find anyone else having three kids. I began to get scared of him doing the things he threatened to do. I lived in fear for a long, long time. There was a lot of bad between us. I think later on in our relationship, we grew apart even though we were married. I think he thought he would always have that hold over me, and the first thing he'd say would be about our kids and he would always make me feel guilty so that I would stay for them. So many things were said. I'm not here to blame him or bash him, but being in a relationship like the one we had was just all bad.

When Covid-19 got really bad, we got about $9,000 in back pay. $9,000 for each of us. That was all bad. We bought a car and would stay in a hotel for days at a time with our kids, and that's when the addiction got really bad. We both had more money than we'd ever had, and we blew right through it. We did get our own apartment, but it was just like it was the last time: We had our own place, and the drug use and selling just got worse and worse. As everyone probably knows, what happens to almost every addict? Death, jail or a rehab. Well, we both did some things we weren't proud of. We had a car, so people would pay us money and drugs to borrow our car. We made money any way we could. Eventually, it all caught up to us. It started with me getting pulled over one night, with one of my sons in the back seat. The cops searched the car and did not find anything, so I thought everything was fine. Tomorrow, it would be like nothing happened. That was just the beginning. I think we were both known by all the town cops for being addicts and dealers. The day after I got pulled over, CYS (Children and Youth Services) showed up at our house. I had always heard horror stories of CYS being involved, but at the beginning, it didn't seem so bad. I also didn't know what that one call to CYS would turn into. A few days later, John got arrested. I will always remember the cop that arrested him saying to me, "You will thank me one day. If I don't arrest him now, you might get that call saying he OD'd." People think cops are awful, but not all cops are bad. Some cops really do try to help. He told us before this to go to rehab and get help, but again we addicts don't think we need rehab, let alone think we have a problem. So, John went to jail, and all I could think was, "what now?" In almost 4 years, we were never apart. Our relationship was all I knew for so long, and then I left with three boys, aged three, two, and one. Again, his family helped as much as they could. They kept my oldest just about every day. They were his grandparents, and I had two other boys, so I just thought they were helping out. At the time, I was grateful for them, but when John went to jail, it didn't mean my addiction stopped. If anything, that's when my addiction was at its worst. For the first time in four years, I was back to being by myself again. I had the freedom to go wherever with whomever without someone telling me, "no," or complaining that I was taking too long. At first, with John being in jail, I felt like I was free in a way. that might sound bad, but for so long I always had to answer to someone and barely could leave the house. Now, I had freedom and didn't feel controlled anymore. However, that wasn't a good thing at all. I got pulled over three times in two months, and each time, charges were filed. Two out of the three times, I had my son with me, I am completely embarrassed to say. As I said before, people think you will change and won't do certain things if you have kids. This is far from the truth. It isn't very good to say, but I lived it. That's what drugs do to you. They make you do things you wouldn't ever think you would do. As much as I regret everything I did and everything that happened, I also know that if those certain things didn't happen, I wouldn't be where I am today. After the last time I got pulled over in Pittsburgh, the cop kept telling me I needed to go to rehab and get help. Obviously, I still didn't think I needed help. Mind you, that morning, four people showed up at my apartment where my kids were sleeping, robbed me, and took all of the money I had (most of it from selling drugs, honestly). I had about $300 left in the bank, which was all my money. After getting pulled over in Pittsburgh, all of that was gone too.

After a few days, CYS showed up again. This time they said I needed to go to rehab. Of course, I tried getting out of it. If I went, I would miss Christmas with my three boys and my youngest was going to turn one, so I would miss that also. I remember my case worker said, "You will always find another excuse for why you can't go," and I will never forget that because she was so right. Even before it got to this point, my family and John's family had a kind of 'intervention' to convince me getting help. They said that they would watch my boys, but I just wasn't ready to get help, and I still did not think I had a problem. I thought that it was under control, but it wasn't. I needed help but it's just so much harder to admit that. I think, especially for women, it is a lot harder than for men to go to rehab and admit they need help. I feel like it's looked down upon more for women because we are the mothers and nurturers. We have this certain image that society sees. In reality, there are just as many female addicts as male. It's just sad that we are less likely to get the help we need. So, with the help of my case manager from CenClear, (FYI, I wouldn't have been able to get through half of the things in my life it wasn't for her and CYS), I got into Alpine Springs rehab. As long as I completed the inpatient 28-day program, I would get my boys right back. John's mom had my oldest, and his sister had my other two. They all made sure my boys had an amazing Christmas, and that my youngest had a first birthday party. I will always be thankful for them for that. They really helped as much as they could while I was gone getting the help I needed. I decided to get on the Vivitrol for my heroin addiction, and I started it the day I got home from rehab, January 6, 2021. I took rehab seriously, but not as seriously as I should have. I knew I was going to get the Vivitrol so, I knew that I couldn't do heroin. I didn't take the time to work on the reasons that I started using it in the first place. John and I were still married at this time. I came home to my old apartment and had all three of my boys home with me. It was such a great feeling, but I messed up by not cutting off the other addicts in my life. I knew I couldn't do heroin so quickly after being home, so I just started doing meth.

I moved into a new apartment in Ridgway shortly after being home from rehab. It is where I live now and it is beautiful. My case worker helped me get into a housing program, so they pay my full rent as long as I don't have an income. Also, I got on programs for my utilities, so I didn't have to pay them. I really don't think I'd be where I'm at now if it wasn't for how much my case worker did for me.

The one thing I did work on a lot in rehab was my self-confidence. Being with John, unfortunately, ruined my self-confidence and self-worth. Once that's lost, sometimes you don't even want to look at yourself in the mirror. I hated myself for so long, but eventually, I realized I was worth so much more, and I deserved so much better than to be called names and put down every day. Just that mental abuse alone is one of the main reasons I would do drugs. The drugs always made me feel better, or at least that's what I told myself. I just wanted to find someone who would appreciate me, not take me for granted, someone who would respect me and do for me what I would do for them. I never thought that I would find someone else. I thought John and I would be married for years, but after rehab, I just decided I couldn't let myself be miserable all the time.

I was still married to John, but on January 26, 2021, I met Nicholas and I will forever be grateful for him coming into my life when he did. I was very open about still being married, having children and being an addict. We became so close so fast. We'd talk on the phone for hours, talk all day every day and he made me feel a way I've never felt before. A few weeks after meeting Nicholas and hanging out a few times I had one of the hardest conversations I've ever had. I finally decided to leave John while he was still in jail. I'll always feel bad for how I left him, but if he hadn't been in jail, I don't think I could have done it. Trust me, I felt awful about having to tell him not only that I didn't want to be together, but that I met someone else. However, I will never regret Nicholas helping me get out of a situation that I was trapped in for so long.

They say that two addicts shouldn't date. Obviously, after being with John, I can see why. Nicholas was also an addict. He was living in a halfway house when we met, and I was only weeks out of rehab. We may not have been the best for each other then, but we just had this connection that neither one of us could let go. He was living with me within about three weeks of knowing each other. Everyone said how I rushed into it too fast, it won't last, but no one could deny how much happier I was, and how great he treated me. We were both addicts, though, so for the first two to three months of being together, we would use meth a lot. We enabled each other at first. After a short time, that whole lifestyle came back. We drove all over to pick up meth, no matter the time or distance. It was like a routine for us, and we both went downhill. Before I knew it, I would go to Drug and Alcohol Abuse Services, and fail the drug tests. Legally, they couldn't tell CYS why I failed, but I did know I wanted to tell them before they found out from someone else. I thought I was doing the right thing at the time. I admitted I was struggling, I admitted Nicholas was struggling. I was maybe a little too honest, but my CYS worker didn't seem too concerned. A few days later, I got a call saying I need to come to the CYS office before they closed that day. I was sick. I knew I wouldn't pass a drug test but I also had to take responsibility for my actions and the things I was doing. They did a mouth swab and I failed for meth, which I also admitted to doing. I had my youngest with me at the time, and I thought if I admitted to what I did, I could go to rehab again and get my kids back like I did before, but that was not at all what happened.

My boys were three, two, and one, and they got removed from my home for safety reasons. I chose for them to be placed with their grandparents until I could have them back. I was told I had to go to rehab again, and would have to do certain things before I could get them back. Until I left, I could still see the boys, but the visits were supervised. That broke my heart. I was really a piece of shit mom, I was selfish. I didn't know how I let things get so bad that I lost my children. They were my world, but I just couldn't choose them over the drugs, and that's a feeling I will have to live with until the day I die. I don't think I will ever fully forgive myself for losing them.

I also never thought their grandparents would file for custody and make things much harder than they already were. John's mom always told me that she "would never try to take custody," but I should never have believed that. I left their son for someone else and I was actually happy. John always told me if I left him that, his parents would take our kids, and I always just laughed and never thought it would happen, but it did. After rehab, I had to follow through with drug and alcohol counseling, and random drug tests, and I could only see my kids once a week for one hour supervised visits at the CYS office. After almost two months of office visits, the visits moved into the community, though still supervised. We would go to the park and my sister would supervise. Eventually, the visits moved back to my house, supervised by CYS, my sister, or the grandparents. I kept being told by CYS I was making progress, and the goal was for them to be back home by the end of August, so that was what I was praying for. Little did I know I got custody papers in the mail and the grandparents filed for full, legal, physical custody.

I was broken. I admit I was in a bad place for a long time, but as soon as it went to the courts, it was a whole different experience. Long story short, CYS closed the case because custody was granted to the grandparents. From here on out, the communication was between lawyers and my ex-husband's parents. It was awkward so many times. I was hurt, embarrassed, and sick that I did this all to myself. I had to do supervised visits for a year before they even agreed to unsupervised visits. My sister would change her work schedule every week to be able to come to my house to supervise so I could see them. She spent every Friday night at my home with her two girls for 4 hours. She never complained. She would move mountains for me if it meant that I would get time with my kids. She truly is an amazing person. This past April, I was finally granted unsupervised visits, and then in the summer, I was able to have them for six hours, three times a week. At the end of July, they started to stay overnight every other Friday. It has been a crazy year and a half. So many times, I wondered "what's the point?" I felt that no matter how hard I tried, I was barely given a chance to be a parent again. All of that anger I had for myself, though, is what helped motivate me to stay sober. I don't get to take my kids to school, play dates, or appointments. I mean, I can go with their grandparents, but it's always an awkward thing because I feel like every place has a copy of our custody order, and knows that I lost my kids. It's a tough thing to deal with sometimes. I blame myself and my addiction. I lost the three boys who mean the most to me.

My kids are now five, four, and two, and I have a 3-month old baby boy with Nicholas. I left rehab on May 12, 2021, and that is when my relationship with Nick really took off. We realized we couldn't live like this anymore. We needed to change, and if one of us couldn't stay sober, then we just weren't meant to be. I will always regret losing my kids, but if that didn't happen, I don't know where I would be. It needed to happen as much as I hate saying that. It made me wake up and reevaluate my whole life. Who should be in my life and who shouldn't? What was important and what wasn't? I hate not having my kids as much as I would like to, but when the judge granted me overnights, that was a big step. Whenever I get upset about my kids, I have to remember I got high for years, and lied about it so many times. I still have a lot of proving myself to do to people. Their grandparents just want that stability for my kids right now, and I will always be thankful to for them giving them a good life. I still get mad and upset about it some days, but I just remember I'm a lot further than I was a year ago. I just have to keep proving to people that I can stay sober, that I can live a sober life. Sober has never felt so good, honestly.

I can't remember the last time that I was in such a good mental state. Nicholas and I had a baby boy on May 11, 2022. His due date was actually May 12, and that's the same day I left rehab in 2021. It's weird how things like that work out sometimes. I believe everything really does happen for a reason. Somedays, being sober is hard, but the longer you are in sobriety, the easier it becomes. I did intensive outpatient drug and alcohol therapy for 3 months, 4 times a week. Over time the sessions decreased, and as of April 2022 I was successfully discharged. I never thought that would happen when I first started. It was a long nine months, but I put in the work. I also had the best therapist. I couldn't have asked for anyone better. He helped me more in my recovery more than he will probably ever know. If you genuinely want to stay sober, you need a good support system. Luckily between my sisters, my therapist, and my case worker I had the absolute best one. I really am living my best life right now. I have my own family now, the family I always wanted. My relationship is the farthest thing from toxic. A lot of people don't realize how much a bad relationship can lead to drug use. I'm in a relationship now where we don't ever fight. We communicate about everything and always tell the truth no matter if it hurts. We are best friends. Nicholas is my biggest supporter. He taught me how to love myself again. I don't think I've ever smiled as much as I smile when were together. He is one of the biggest blessings that God sent into my life. When I found out I was pregnant with our son, we were both early in recovery, about 4 months which is still very early, so there was definitely a lot of anxiety about having a baby on top of both of us just learning how to live sober.

I mean, I have three other boys but with my son Rylen, it just feels different. Motherhood feels different. Nicholas works everyday so that I can stay home with him, and so that I can get my other three boys when I'm allowed. I'm just happy now. Things feel right. When you are doing the right thing, things will eventually work out. I am currently on house arrest for when I got pulled over in Pittsburgh in 2020 and let me tell you, it's tough some days. At least I get to be home with my baby and I still get to be a mother. Initially, I was supposed to do four months in jail & 4 months on house arrest, but the judge saw documented proof of how far I'd come in a year, and how amazing my progress was, so he let me do eight months on house arrest, which is such a blessing. I go to probation weekly and not having to walk in there with the anxiety of failing a drug test is a whole different type of feeling. I'm not exactly where I want to be yet, but I'll get there. The other day I actually took my car to the garage to get inspected, and that's the first time Nicholas and I have ever even brought a car to a garage, let alone had the money to pay for it. We have priorities now and things that are more important than using. I have such a good relationship with my family, they love Nicholas, and have always treated him like part of the family, just like his mother does for me. Neither of us had the best relationships with our families, and now finally, we are both closer than ever with them. It is so nice.

Getting sober doesn't happen overnight. You may stop using. Putting down the drugs is only the first step, but it's a start. There is hope for every struggling addict out there. You may get sober and relapse and have to start over, but so what? At least you are trying. Changing your life at first is like a full-time job, but once you make the change and things start falling into place, you'll soon realize you don't need drugs to feel good or make things better. I'll always be an addict, but I'm finally at the good part of my life.

One day at a time.

~**Kelsey**

"MISSION IMPOSSIBLE"

"MISSION IMPOSSIBLE"

My name is Dylan, I am 26 years old and I am from Brandy Camp, Pennsylvania. And this is my Story.

This is a story of myself, my life, and the demons that surround me, which I also call addiction. Addiction is a disease, for which there is no known cure. Beating addiction is like defying impossible odds. Like many others in this world, I have lived and struggled with addiction for many years. And the reality of this disease is frightening, very few survive, the rest won't make it. That is the sad truth.

Like every other story, my story has a purpose. The purpose is to make a difference in someone else's life. Through honesty, hope, and experience, my goal is to tell my story in hopes of helping another person. Whether it's the addict themselves, a loved one, or an individual struggling to understand addiction, I believe my story can help make a difference in saving others from the pain, time, and suffering caused by the disease of addiction. I will focus on telling my story by answering a question; a question many of us find discomforting; a question that doesn't seem logical, and might even be seen as insane. It took me years and a lot of pain for me to answer.

My answer is, "Yes."

I truly believe it's the only reason I can share my story with others today. It's the only reason I am breathing, and the only reason I can share my hope and wisdom with others.

So, ask yourself, "Is it possible for the thing that broke you down and tore you apart to be the same thing that puts you back together?" "Can heroin addiction, the same thing that nearly took my life, be the same thing that SAVED it?"

The answer to that question is "Yes," in regards to my own story. I am determined to share how and why that answer has given me life today.

I was born in Dubois, PA, and raised in Elk County my entire life. From the very start, I had hopes and dreams just like every other kid growing up. I was surrounded by a loving family and many friends. My immediate family included my father, grandfather, half-sister and my mother. (who also happens to be my best friend). Even though most kids set their hopes and dreams high, I happened to set mine even higher. Being from Elk County, my family and friends have always spent most of their time outdoors, with dirt bikes and four-wheelers included. We were always riding with the locals, and I began riding around the age of 5. However, my life would change forever in the fall of 2005, when I was 8 years old. Me and my parents went to Steel City Pro Motocross National in Delmont, Pennsylvania. To this day, I can recall the sight, the smells and the feelings of butterflies in my stomach. Throughout the weekend, I was surrounded by the smell of race fuel and dirt bikes. I got the chance to meet the best riders in the world and see the world from their perspective. They were surrounded by family,

"MISSION IMPOSSIBLE"

fame, and fortune and they got all that by doing what they loved to do. I remember leaving that weekend in the back of the car and telling myself, "I am going to be a professional Motocross rider, that is what I am going to do!"

From that moment on, I set my mind to do whatever it took to accomplish my dreams. My parents surprised me one day with my first dirt-bike, and I began teaching myself the harder concepts of riding. We began going to local races and then races all around Pennsylvania. My parents bought me every motocross game and I watched every movie video on the internet. I would often spend countless house underneath my parents' porch in the dirt playing with my toy dirt-bikes while my dad worked in the garage. Around the age of 10, we began traveling to bigger races, qualifiers, and nationals, up and down the east coast. While I was devoting my life to motocross, I still tried my best to get my education in school. My favorite teacher was a math teacher. Everyone knew I hated school, but he understood why. Every Friday he would ask "Where we racing this weekend?" And I recall a conversation where he told me to always follow your dreams, no matter how crazy they might seem.

I felt the odds were stacked against me, and I challenged that. Around 2011, I was progressing rapidly, but yet I had thoughts of giving up. I didn't think I could beat the odds and I became frustrated with the struggles. However, I failed to realize what lay ahead of me. And, in 2012, my dreams became a reality. I was 15 when I moved to the big bikes, and something evolved in me mentally, physically and spiritually. I focused myself and began to follow my heart. I would ride every day and often dress myself in two sweatshirts, jeans and ride my mountain bike in 90-degree weather up and down local roads. I got myself in shape and put whatever I had left into chasing my dreams. I want to add that in these years, I also focused on being a kid and living life on life's terms. I did drink lots of alcohol, chased girls, partied, smoked pot and even experimented with cocaine. Over the years I witnessed many dirt biker's riders fail and they never even had the chance to live a "normal life. I wanted different, and It seemed to work. By the middle of 2012, I was racing on a Pro-Am level and winning races all around the country. I had a fan base at the racetracks and people rooting for me back at home. My confidence was at an all-time high and it seemed I was about to live my best life. Right before the beginning of each race, my Dad would give me a knuckle touch and tell me "just have fun." My grandfather was my biggest fan and each race would tell me, "don't kill yourself, this is just for fun." I always assured him I wouldn't and reluctantly agreed with him. However, I lied to them each and every time. My intentions were to win, and I would die trying! In 2013, while racing at the Amateur National Regionals in Budds creek, Maryland. I qualified for the Amateur Nationals in Hurricane Mills, Tennessee. It is called Loretta Lynn's and means I was one of the fastest 42 rides in the country at the Pro-Am Level. It is here where careers are established and dreams are made. My dreams were on their way, at least, I thought so. The following week is what I consider the pivot point in my story.

On August 1st, 2013, A week before Loretta Lynn's, my life changed forever. I was arrested for DUI after leaving a party, and was sent to a juvenile detention lock up. That was my first night sleeping in a jail cell and I no longer had an idea of what the future held for me. After going to court, the reality set in. I realized my years of racing was over, and quite possibly my dreams. I was sent to juvenile lock up for six to nine months. Prior to getting locked up, I was in a relationship with my teenage sweetheart and we had a strong relationship. After two months of being away, she informed me that she was pregnant and we were having a baby girl. Even though I was aware that it would be difficult, I devoted the time that I was locked up to focusing on my return home to racing and to becoming a dad. I continued to follow Motocross and still remained faithful to my dreams. I often spent my time reading Motocross magazines and a book titled *"What to Expect When You're Expecting."* After nearly eight months, I was excited to come home and pick up where I left off with racing and with my new addiction, a daughter. However, returning home proved way more challenging than I anticipated. I was informed that my daughter wasn't mine, and returning to racing and home life was a culture shock. While locked up, I was surrounded by inner city kids and I was in a different world that I came to understand. I struggled to adapt to being home and felt isolated. I began drinking and smoking a lot. Nearly every day. I barely made it through 11th and 12th grade. I began selling drugs and experimenting with every drug possible. I surrounded myself with money, drugs, negative people and I lost all my focus and faith. It was in this moment I made what I consider the biggest mistake of my life.

Three months after I came home was the first time I used heroin. I'll never forget the comforting feeling and the sigh of relief the first time I used. I often tell people that injecting heroin is like a sexual climax while dropping off a roller coaster, with a warm rush flowing throughout your whole body. It became the answer in my life, as it does with most addicts. It helped me understand and also it helped block reality. It became my love and it became the simplest form of sanity, at least that's what I thought. Soon it became a problem, and a constant fight to stay well. Eventually, I no longer felt the initial rush, and I made the decision to let go. The only problem was I couldn't, no matter how hard I tried or how much it effected my life. I have spent time in four different rehabs. I have done over six years combined, between five different county jails and nine different state prisons. I have watched my professional racing career disappear right before my eyes. It has become a love - hate relationship. I have lost so many friends to heroin overdose. September 10th, 2017, after injecting heroin, I suffered a severe overdose. I lay on the porch surrounded by my mom, girlfriend and two friends who were trying to revive me. I was not breathing, and I didn't have an active pulse for nearly seven minutes. The two doses of Narcan did nothing for me, and it wasn't until after the EMT'S electrically shocked me that my heart began beating again on its own. I spent 33 months in state prison because of my overdose. And what was the first thing I did when I got home from the hospital? I shot up more heroin. It was a never-ending fight and it was a never-ending thought. I know as you read this, my question from the beginning seems unthinkable, and my answer can't possibly have an explanation. So how did addiction pull me back to life? How could something so evil be so bold that it helped me survive and bring me back to life?

Well, I am a big believer in "what doesn't kill you can make you stronger." In the midst of my addiction, I endured extreme highs and extreme lows. A lot of addicts will often question when they hit bottom. I don't believe in a moment of rock bottom and I don't believe in the word, "recover". Heroin addiction will cause a fake sense of highs and lows, and the only definition of rock bottom would be your life being taken away completely. In my experience, you can never be recovered, you can, however, be in recovery. Addiction is something that can't be cured, it's a lifelong disease. You can be in recovery and maintain sobriety, but the thought can always arise. Heroin has taken nearly everything from me. The time and pain it has caused me prevented me from exploring many things that life has to offer. More than once I lay on the floor screaming for help because I was suffering from extreme opioid constipation. I would regularly go two, three, four weeks without using the bathroom. More than once I lay naked, rolling on the floor of a jail cell, dry heaving and sweating profusely. Often, there were weeks of me hallucinating, shaking, and pleading for death. Heroin has given me everything, while the same time given me nothing. The life it has brought me has made me overcome extreme adversity time and time again. I often tell people it could always be worse, you can be dope sick. If you can get past being dope sick you can do anything. I once said "If I can get past the sickness, I can conquer anything I put my mind to." People fail to realize that life isn't just a walk in the park. Its filled with obstacle and choices. And nobody is perfect, people make mistakes. It's how you overcome these mistakes, how you learn from them. Throughout the years, addiction has taken nearly everything from me, but it forced me to think, and learn. And I have come to believe that knowledge and learning are the two biggest components of survival. Life is unpredictable, and every day could always be your last. If life was always ups, then you would never have to overcome obstacles or be given a chance to learn. With addiction providing me more downs, it has forced me to overcome more. It has taught me that I only have one life.

There was a point in my life where I wished death upon myself. I attempted suicide by drugs more than once. I wanted life to be nothing but easy, and I didn't want to have

"MISSION IMPOSSIBLE"

to overcome anything. I didn't want to learn to vice life, I just wanted it given to me.

Each time addiction didn't kill me, it forced me to move on. And each time I moved on, I learned something new. And each time I learned something new, I understood more about life. And the more I understood life, the more desire I had to live it. And the more desire I had to live, the more I was reminded who I am. Reminding myself who I am creates room for more.

When I look into the mirror now, I love what I see. I allow myself to smile, and I constantly remind myself of what I have overcome and what I have been through. I tell myself, **"If you spend too much time looking back, you might trip looking forward."** Never forget who you are, what defines you and what your dreams are. My dreams are to become a father, and to share my knowledge, to become successful in whatever I have decide to take on. Just because one dream is gone, doesn't mean I will give up on the others. Nobody should ever let addiction define them. You can allow it to help you overcome more. Understand that what works for one person may not work for others. Allow yourself to move on and learn from every curveball life might throw at you. Allow yourself to grow.

I want to send my regards to every addict out there. Or anyone who suffers because a loved one is struggling with addiction. My heart goes out to each and every one of you. Unfortunately, life is filled with ups and downs. But I truly believe it's better that way. It gives us humans a chance to grow and a need to overcome.

This is my story.

Thanks for taking the time to read it.

With hopes and wisdom

~ **Dylan**

"MISSION IMPOSSIBLE"

faith over fear

"It's not the scars we live with, but it's their instances we live through"

— DAMION LIPINSKI

Just the same it's not just the oppositions' in our life that condemn the future by unforgiving the past, self-destruction also comes by unforgiving. So, to heal and start recover from the past I had to forgive and let go of that past.

But before that pivotal moment in my life, I would like to take you back to 10/30/76 the day I was born. I had scared life before I even entered this world.

My mother was an addict and used while she was pregnant. I am pretty sure I was born into this world and addict. My father and mother had separated before I was born. One day my father came to see me and found me found me in my crib, I hadn't been changed in days. I had diaper rash so bad that my skin was peeling off. My dad said it was the last straw and he took me that day. I lived with my dad for the first 10 years of my life. So, I don't remember much about my mother, even though she would come around once in a while. It was never for very long.

My grandfather had a pizza shop and my dad worked for him. One time my mother came in there while he was working, I was there because I was too young to go to school. My dad got real upset and made her leave. She wasn't clean and was not allowed to be around me. I remember seeing her and I think I knew who she was, I was so young that my memory is a little blurry. But I felt as if I knew her, I think I may have recognized her or maybe I felt connected in some way?

I don't remember many bad things, only what I have been told. I am thankful for that, *because* what I had seen was enough that screwed me up when I got older.

No child should have to go through this kind of life.

But this is a little background to my life before addiction:

I had a pretty normal childhood, I had dad, step mom, step brothers. All the way up to the age of 10, as a kid I did some dumb things, I had some behavioral issues. As it got worst my step mom became more distance away from me. She started to isolate me from the rest of the family. Making him punish me more. Showed a lot of favoritism with the other kids. Eventually, she made him to choose, me or them.

Of course, he chose them. It threw my world upside down. He told me that I had to move in with my maternal grandmother. He promised me he would come and see me. But I knew it wasn't true in my heart. I had to say goodbye to everything I knew at the time. I was so sad and heart broken. I would lay at night and look at the window and curse God, as I was sitting there as a child broken hearted, the tears streaming down my cheeks. I was asking God, WHY? Why did you make my dad leave me? Why don't I have a mom? Why me?

I didn't have a great relationship with God anyway. However, I was raised Catholic, I went to the catholic school, I went to church. So, I did have some understanding of God. And I was angry at him for what was going on in my life. I was so young and didn't understand what was wrong with me.

I turned away from God, I turned away from a lot of things. I turned that hurt to angry. It begun to snowball. I started acting out. I started smoking pot, I started to drink at the age of 12. I was put into foster care a few times which added to my anger.

I will say, I am so grateful for my grandmother. She remained the rock in my life, she took me to church, Methodist church. Even though I wasn't ready to forgive God or let him in, the seeds were planted. And eventually they would grow, but not for a while. I had more to experience, I had more to understand.

My heart hurts to this day for the pain that I caused my grandmother.

Living the life of addiction was worse yet, I had a broken heart, a broken spirit. It was fueled by anger, deception, betrayal, and broken trust.

Needless to say, I spent my time in juvenile detention.

At age 14, I stole a car and was on a high-speed chase, with multiple police cars chasing me, until I finally wrecked and they pulled me out of the car.

I was sentenced to a year in juvenile again. When it was time to be released, my case workers tried to help me find some kind of family support. I had burned a lot of bridges. But we reached out to my other grandparents on my father's side so I would have a place to go when I was released.

They were happy to help out and let me stay there. The problem is, even in juvie, they didn't offer me any mental health help. I had no one to talk to help guide me out of that.

I tried to commit suicide, I had locked myself in the bathroom and sliced my wrist. I was trying to bleed out the pain that I was in. I almost succeed. I wanted to die at that time, I didn't know how else to get rid of all the emotional pain I was in. There was so much; my father abandoning me, my mother not wanting me, and on top of all that my uncle molested me when I was staying with my grandmother. So, yeah, I was full of anger, resentment, pain, shame, and betrayal. I just wanted it to stop, I wanted it to go away, I wanted to go away. I kept it all hidden away.

I stayed with my grandparents for about eight months, but they couldn't help me and I couldn't stay there anymore. My grandmother was ill, she had a heart condition, and I was just too much for them. So, when I was released from the hospital from my suicide attempt, I ended up going to a group home in Pittsburgh. I was huffing, and doing all kind of drugs, just to escape the pain. I ran away from the group home and I was in front of the judge again, and he said, "Done. You need to serve out your sentence." I did two years.

I got out in 1995, I was eighteen, I weighed 260lbs, and I was 6'1". I was in Pittsburgh, my home town. But I came out with an attitude. I was cocky, I was working out all the time while I was locked up.

This was the beginning of my bigger drug problem. I started smoking weed all the time, LSD, and cocaine. Then I got into selling drugs and joined a gang which opened up a whole new world of activity to me. I guess I realized how much I didn't care when I started to carry a gun all the time. It was just a high scale of violence that I felt eventually it would be the end of me. I would either end up dead or in prison for killing someone.

We started to rob other drug dealers. We robbed people, then we did home invasions. We never thought twice about any of it. This was the world I created, this was where I felt comfortably numb. Maybe it was partly the thrill of it all that made me feel something? I am not sure, but it is where I felt I belonged.

I remember getting into a bad fight on the south side in 1997. It was supposed to be a one on one, but there were about 15 of them and three of us. We got beat down pretty bad, but my buddies left me there, my back was up against the wall and I was alone.

I think I was just waiting for my end. I would consume large amounts of coke or any other drug. I was always first in line! If we robbed a house, I was the first one to go in. I just didn't care anymore. I was daring death.

I ended up getting arrested in 1998 for armed robbery in New Orleans. I was looking at some major time, 10 years to 199 years, can't lie, that shook me up bad. I first got into the New Orleans parish prison, which is a pretty bad place to be. I was coming off of drugs, I was so sick, and I knew I had done something really wrong. I didn't know where my life was going, I didn't what my future looked like now. I was going to do some major time.

I had no problem adapting to this life, spending as much time as I did in juvenile and other jail time. This was something I could handle, I was comfortable around the other inmates.

As my withdrawals got better, I started to wonder where my life was going to? Where was I heading? I wasn't thinking about recovery or anything like that, I just had no clue to where or what I was doing. I didn't even think about praying. Talking to God was completely out of my realm. It is funny that there was nobody there who talked to you about anything, not God, not recovery, not hope. It was like an abyss, complete silence.

As I got closer to my sentence they transferred me to a different part of the prison. I was right across from this big guy, a biker from Texas, he was about 6'7" and about 300lbs. He had all kind of tattoos all over him. He was in there for four counts of murder. I didn't know this at the time, I was just being cool, playing chess and hanging out.

Well, I got to talking to him and I asked him if he wanted to cell up? (This is what we refer to as bidding.) The guy said, well you will have to talk to the lieutenant. I put a request in to talk to them and I told them I wanted to move into my brother's cell. I said, "his name is Doug Witney." They said, "Are you serious? Do you know who he is?" He is here for four counts of murder! One being a child, the other being the child's mother, and the other two were adult males. He brutally murdered these people." They said "ok, sign this waver!"

But I couldn't say no, for some odd reason I felt I needed to be with him. I won't lie about it, I was nervous, I could figure it out, but it was something I knew I needed to do.

It wasn't long and we started talking about what he did and what I did. There were times I was a little unsettled. It was a time that my life took a turn, right before I moved in with him. I prayed this prayer that I knew I would never forget. I hadn't accepted Christ yet, but he knew I would later and He knew He had plan for me.

I prayed "God, if you get me out of this and see me through this, I don't know what is going to happen, please have mercy on me. I don't want anything out of it" and I continued to make all kind of deals with God, we all know you can't make deals with God, I felt that he was up there listening to me and laughing. But I knew what I was searching for, in my heart of hearts, and in my mind. As I stood there holding on to those steel bars, I knew why I was there. I had a broken heart, a broken family. I said, God, please if you can give me one thing, a family. I want a wife and children. One that can't be taken away, or one I can walk away from.

Now I was back in the cell with Douglas. Big Doug. He asked me to hold back and not go out to the day room, I want you to sit down and talk. So, I did, Doug was able to get cigarettes and we were allowed to smoke at that time. I never had money from my commissary because I didn't have any family to leave me any. Neither did Doug, but he had talent, he was an amazing artist, so he would draw portraits of people and they would pay him.

So, he sits backs and says Look, "I know that you get commissary and you never offer me anything" I started getting angry, he was pulling me up on the truth. My cousin would give me money once in a while. Doug knew this, I could feel my self-getting all puffed up. Until he said, "Wait, just sit down" then he went on to explain. "It isn't about materialistic things, it's about respect." I sat down and started to listening to him. He started to explain to me what it is like to be a man. A man is only man when he learns to love himself and be honest with himself. If you can't, then you cannot be honest or love anyone else. As we sat there talking and getting deeper into the discussion. I started to realize, I was 19 years old, and I was looking at 199 years. I didn't know who I was, and I didn't know what was going to happen to me. I realized that I wasn't being honest with myself. I think Doug could see that in me and he knew. He was a man of God and he would tell me some stories. He said he was in the prison in Texas when they started to integrate African Americans in. It used to be separate; whites on one side, African Americans on the other. He said it got ugly, a lot of riots and fights. He said they had "turnkeys," they were inmates that carried keys to help the guides. He said this one time a riot was going on and he was running down the hall trying to escape, when a turnkey opened the door and said, "Come this way." He went in, and the door closed and locked. He turned around and there was no body there. He knew then he was being saved for something more. He was a firm believer in angels and in God.

I don't know a lot of his circumstances, but what I do know is he was a man of God. It is because of him that I started to search God out. He told me, tonight when you lay down in bed, he said "I want you to think about your life, go all the way back, back to the first bad memory you have. When you come to the first bad memory you have, think what could you have done to change it?" It really made me think about where my life would be if I had done things differently. It also made me think about my future more. It made me think about my future decisions, and about how I could have done things differently. He knew what he was doing, he knew it would make me think. He told me, "You have two choices, you can either get through this and be man, or you can continue not to grow into that man, to walk around with a chip on your shoulder. Then you will not make it out of here. This will be your life; prison.

This was in 1998, in New Orleans, the murder capital at that time. There were gang wars, the heroin epidemic, and a lot of poverty. Young people were coming in every day from every parts of the city.

After 18 months of waiting, my sentencing day came. I was sitting there getting ready to be sentenced, I had a public defender, of course. He read off my charges, I was holding my breath. The Judge finally spoke, and said: "By the power vested in me by the State of Louisiana, I sentence you to ten years in the state correctional prison."

"MISSION IMPOSSIBLE"

My gut fell to the floor, but I know it could have been worse. I was looking at a possible 198 years, but ten years to a 19-year-old kid felt like a life time. Being sentenced in a state where you have no friends or family was tough. I was alone.

They moved me around a lot, in the beginning, from one state holding prison to another. I know some of you may not understand this, but I was moved back and forth from West and East Carroll, which are all a part of the New Orleans detention center.

In 2001, I was out in the yard at East Carroll, they had this make shift tub out in basketball court. They asked if anyone wanted to get Baptized. I wanted to jump right up and say, "YES, ME!", but I couldn't. I sat there and the preacher asked again. I still didn't move. I felt everything in my body saying, "Get up and do it!" But, I didn't. Then the preacher asked for the final time, "Are you sure? Doesn't anyone want to get baptized?" I jumped up and said "YES! I do!" I ran over and wanted to jump in the tub, and he helped me in to the tub. The preacher told me he was proud of me, and that this was what God wanted for me. He baptized me in the name of the Father, Son and the Holy Spirit. When I came out of that water, I knew I was a new man. I knew the old man died and I was coming out brand new. Something changed in me, I felt it deep inside me. But that was only the beginning of what God had in store for me.

Being human, I still felt the desire, once in a while, to get high. So, I smoked some pot. It wasn't in His plan and I felt it.

Of course, it wasn't easy and I still struggled. God needed me to work on myself. I worked on my spirit with the Holy Spirit. I went to church and read the Bible. Where I was, there was no support for recovery, there were no NA programs, or anything else that helped people to work on recovery. We were more or less just thrown into there to serve time for the wrongs we did, and offered no hope for growth or rehabilitation. We were all left to figure things out for ourselves. I relied on God to help me through those times, but I knew I needed more. I knew I needed to address all the trauma; from childhood, trauma from my teen years, trauma from the abuse, neglect, and abandonment. I knew I was broken and that is why I was there, stripped down to my naked self, soul exposed to God. I knew I had to right my wrongs, so that I could feel whole again.

I got out in 2006 and I moved in with my grandmother. I started going to church, working a job. I was out in the world again and with the world's temptations. I had not worked my recovery and, yes, you know what happened. I started drinking and then of course one thing lead to another, and I was getting high again. I was drifting back to the life I wanted to forget. I was drifting back into that darkness.

"MISSION IMPOSSIBLE"

The unthinkable happened then. I was in a horrible car accident. I was life flighted. I had broken my back. I was in and out of the hospital. In 2010, I had more surgery on my back. I became addicted to pain pills, which lead to me to heroin.

The first time I used heroin, I shot up. That is what I did for the next two years, it didn't matter where I got it from, as long as I was able to get high.

I eventually ended back up in jail in 2012 for three misdemeanors. the Judge in Jefferson county wasn't messing around. He hammered me, and I ended up getting 5 to 12 years in SCI Fayette County Prison. The day I got there, they were flying out two prison guards, SWAT was there, and the whole place was on lock down. We were in lock down for two weeks.

My PTSD kicked in from my first time in prison. It was six months before my parole down in Louisiana, and I was in a riot. It was bad, they took guards as hostages and tortured them. I really thought I was going to die. My friend, Davy, took me in and had me sit on his bunk so nobody would mess with me. He told me, "Don't worry, I got this."

I don't think I can express the fear you have when something like this is going on. The prisoners don't care who they hurt, what they do, and who is in the line of fire. You had all kinds of inmates in there, from all walks of life. There were people who had killed children, raped woman, murdered people. There were violent predators who had no value for human life, and who were full of hatred. So here I was, walking into a prison on lock down. Not a good place to be.

Fast forward:

I got out of my prison sentence in 2019. I knew when I got out that I needed to work my recovery. I heard about NA and AA programs. I realized how important working my recovery was. I had to do this as part of my parole.

I will say, I think NA helped me, but I didn't like calling myself an addict. How is a person able to change if they keep referring to themselves as an addict? I expressed that, and I understand it was just the term that is used.

I quit and started going to a Program called SMART, which stands for Self-Management and Recovery Training. SMART is science based and it made sense to me. I became a facilitator. We had different groups called "Inside Out," which were rookie police officers come in and we would have an open discussion. Sometimes, we would have 50 people attend these meetings. We would sit and talk about how we perceive them, and they could share their thoughts about us. We talked about solutions and ideas about how to break down all the stigma between us. I learned a lot of good things!

However, if you don't understand addiction, you just don't understand how easy it is to slip back into that old life. I got out of prison, and the guy I was in prison with lived right next door. Of course, we both went back down that path, again. We were doing meth, heroin or whatever we could get our hands on. I hated myself and everything else. I turned on everyone. I ripped up and broke stuff in the house, I was just horrible. I was ruining my family again.

I am in recovery again and I thank God every day. I wake up in the morning and the first thing I do is thank God. I read my Bible, I go to church, and I work my recovery. I put all my anger, all my fears and pain at the cross. I give it to Christ. I know that everyone has a path to follow, I know that without God in my life, that I would not be here today. I know I have a problem. I had to learn my lesson the hard way, but I believe that it was God who saved me, and is keeping me here for a reason. I am learning to live my life sober again. I am being honest with myself, but I am being honest with God.

This is my personal story, I want you to know there is hope. Reach out to someone, reach out to love, reach out to Christ. I hope that my story inspires you and my prayer for you is that you never give up. God loves you, and so do I.

~ **Damion Lipinski**

- On a Biblical note. If you hear something three times, pay attention. It is often a message that you need to hear and take to heart.
- According to google: Louisiana is still the prison capital of the world. https://www.nola.com/news/

crime_police/article_8feef59a-1196-5988-9128-1e8e7c9aefda.html
- Information on the SMART Program https://community.smartrecovery.org/community/
- Also, NA Narcotics Anonymous: https://www.na.org/meetingsearch/

"MONSTERS ARE REAL AND THEY'RE TRAINED HOW TO KILL"

LYRICS BY "SHINEDOWN"

Some say "pot" is the gateway drug, which I always found amusing. I believed that alcohol and nicotine were, because most kids start off by drinking and smoking cigarettes. Well, we are all wrong. According to "Kanwarpal Dhaliwal," TRAUMA is the gateway drug. If you truly listen to an addict's story with your heart, not just your ears, you will feel the trauma they were born into, the gateway drug that is overlooked by us all.

"MONSTERS ARE REAL AND THEY'RE TRAINED HOW TO KILL"

From the time I was 16 years old until about 25, I was known as a "party girl." Wherever there was alcohol, you would find me. This is how I met Michael. He was the "party boy" who just wanted to have fun. Of course we clicked, we were two of a kind! Shortly after meeting, we became girlfriend and boyfriend. About six months later my partying days had to come to an end. Yep, I got pregnant.

On September 20, 1994, our beautiful daughter was born. My mom was livid that she wasn't a boy. She looked at me and said, "A girl, huh? Are you going to send her back?" I just glared at her. Then she said, "I hope she is THREE times worse than you ever were!" Then the door opened and the nurse brought the baby in. She was crying so hard and was going horse. I will never forget her screams. The doctor came in a little later and told me she had heart problems and were sending her to the DuBois NICU. Then he just walked out like nothing was happening.

I could barely sleep that night. I must've dozed off because I was woken up by the ringing of a telephone. I was so scared to answer it. It was too early to be any family. I asked God for strength and I answered, "Hello, Ms. Smith? This is Dr Siar from the DuBois NICU. You have one strong little girl here. We almost lost her THREE times, but she is one heck of a fighter nothing is ever going to keep her down." I then asked him how her heart was and he didn't know what I meant by that. He said, "She doesn't have heart problems! She was born with Strep B in her lungs." They were going to keep her for ten days. I was released after THREE days and stayed with her the rest of the time. And what did I name this beautiful girl? Brooke. My little babbling Brooke.

We lived with my parents and I was so beyond grateful for that. I had never even babysat before. As Brooke kept getting older, she became more and more attached to my parents. Sometimes I got jealous because it seemed like they were the parents and I was just the babysitter, but I just went with it.

As a baby, Brooke was always sick with infected sinuses, double ear infections, and high fevers. It seemed as if our second home was the doctor's office! One of her many sicknesses was different. I couldn't get her fever down and it just felt as if she was burning up. I was sitting in the recliner rocking her, so that she could sleep. I just sat there and listened to her breathe. Something just wasn't right. My dad came over and took her for a little bit. Then all of a sudden Brooke started to tremble. I was so scared! I didn't know what to do so my dad told me to call 911. When the paramedics got there, they checked her over and said that she had a seizure. They wanted to admit her to the hospital for observation. While the ambulance was backing down our driveway, the paramedic started tapping on her foot. THREE times than a pause, THREE times then a pause. "C'mon little one stay with us", he said. Then he said, "Phew, she's just in a very deep sleep. That's common after a seizure." At the hospital, they did a bunch of tests and x-rays and admitted her at THREE in the morning. I heard this little tiny voice say, "Mama!" I opened my eyes and I saw Brooke standing up in the crib, smiling from ear-to-ear. I then knew she was ok. The doctor told me later on that she had a "febrile seizure." Sometimes they happen when the fever spikes up too fast.

Michael lived with us for a few months after that and then he moved back with his friends. We attempted to stay together but we were always arguing and fighting. We became more distant and he lost interest in his daughter. When Brooke was two years old, Michael decided to move back to Illinois with his Grandmother. I knew that day would be the last time we would see him, and I was right. A few years after he left, he and his friend were killed in a car accident.

As Brooke got older, she turned into a tomboy. No frilly dresses and dolls for this girl! That's ok, she had her cousin, Ben with her all the time. They loved to play outside, ride their bikes and power wheels, then later on, 4-wheelers. They grew up like siblings instead of cousins.

Right before Brooke's fourth birthday, I met someone. Larry was his name. He was everything I ever wanted. He loved Brooke just as much as his THREE kids. Soulmates we were. Within THREE months we were engaged, six months later we were married. It seemed like the perfect dream! He adopted Brooke, I was so happy she had a dad, and a good one at that! A few months later I wanted another child. It took THREE months to become pregnant. I had another daughter, Emilee. There are seven years between her and

Brooke so they were never close like sisters growing up and to this day they still aren't. Little did I know that the marriage was going to be 16 years of complete hell, and I dragged my daughters down into the deep, dark pit with me.

You see, Larry was an addict. His "Brompton Cocktail" consisted of benzos, pain pills, and alcohol. So, what did this wonderful concoction bring to the family? Jails, institutions, overdoses, and near death. It is one hundred percent true what is said in the rooms of NA. This turned me into a monster! I was beyond angry all the time. I would take my anger out on my girls, screaming and yelling like a lunatic because of where I was keeping us.

Brooke's school days were pretty interesting. Her first-grade teacher would call me to tell me that Brooke had a loud booming voice, and, could I tell her to tone it down because it echoed down the hallways? She faked talking goofy to get into speech therapy because one of her friends had speech therapy, and would come back to class with candy, stickers or some kind of little toy.

Junior high was pretty calm until the eighth grade. Brooke almost got herself expelled because she wrote something obscene about a teacher and the Principal on the bathroom stall. The Principal was all about expelling her. During the meeting, I started crying and the all of our traumas came spilling out. I told them how horrible her home life was. Even the Principal started to cry. She changed her mind about expelling Brooke and used another kind of discipline.

"MONSTERS ARE REAL AND THEY'RE TRAINED HOW TO KILL"

When she started high school, Brooke wanted to get into sports. She played softball and basketball. When Brooke turned fifteen, she started asking me about getting a job. She wanted to start saving for a car. I told her it was either a job or sports, that she couldn't do both. So, she chose a job. I hired her at the restaurant I worked at. When she turned sixteen, she started pounding the hours. Most weeks she worked 32 hours and went to school. Her grades were starting to drop, so I told her I would have to cut her hours back. She got pretty upset and started ranting about how she needed the money. She needed a car and insurance. This is when she started drinking on the weekends. To help her stay awake for school, she began using "Adderall" that she bought from classmates and people she worked with. I had no clue what was going on. I once caught her smoking in the parking lot at work and dragged her home. She threatened to kill herself so I took her to the emergency room and had her admitted to a mental health unit. When she came home, it was the same old song and dance. There was more anger, drugs, and hell. One night she came out of her bedroom with a baseball bat. I swear she was going to use Larry's head as the baseball. She began to hate him, and really, I couldn't blame her.

The day she graduated from high school, I found out she had been a Eucharistic Minister. I was so surprised and proud. Afterwards I asked her, "Why didn't you tell me about this?" and her response was her famous; "I don't know it's no big deal, mom" After we got back home, Brooke went into her room and she stayed in there for a while. When her door opened, there she stood with a bunch of bags. She told me she was moving to Grammy's. My heart sank and I begged her not to go. I told her that I was filing for a divorce and she said, "yeah mom, I heard that one before. That's why he's still here." Then she said that I chose him over her, and she left. At the age of 18, her drinking got worse and the use of Adderall turned into the use of pain pills. By the time she was 19, she knew she was an alcoholic.

In 2016, I filed for a divorce for the THIRD time. I guess the saying, "the third time is the charm" is right! Brooke didn't want to hear about it because I had cried "wolf" before. So, on the day the divorce became finalized, I actually took the papers to her and said, "It's finally over." By this time, different pills and alcohol weren't doing much for her anymore. She started doing anything she could get her hands on to get high.

The year 2017 was the worst year of my life so far. It was the year everything crashed and burned for Brooke. Emilee was fifteen and became pregnant, my dog got killed by a car, and then there was trauma with my mother. She was a breast cancer survivor, but ten years later it came back with a vengeance. For 17 years off and on, she fought this horrible demon. I talked to her every day. The last time I talked to her as my mother was the night before her last chemo appointment. She ended up in the hospital because her white blood cell count and oxygen levels were too low for her treatment.

Well, she went into the hospital my mother and came out with full blown dementia! It got worse and worse, so dad had to admit her to the hospital for memory care. Brooke would go there every morning after work, and sit with her until she went to physical therapy. While my mom was in the hospital, she caught pneumonia. She was transferred over to Pinecrest, which is a nursing home. Brooke continued going to see her every morning. Brook would take her something small that she liked, like a cappuccino, breakfast sandwich, or a donut. Anything little and meaningful to mom. Brooke was now doing heroin but she still wanted to be with her Grandmother.

On October 14, 2017, the hospital called me and said that my mother was passing. I told them I would be right over, but they told me she would be gone by the time I got there. I called Brooke and told her to meet me there. The nurse was right, Mom passed before I got there. Brooke came in a few minutes after me and when I saw the look on Brooke's face, I just held her tight and we both began to cry. This became the start of my worst nightmare and Brooke's one-way ticket to hell. I just lost my mother and now I was about to lose my daughter as well.

Brooke started to crash and burn. First, she lost her job. She called me up crying, and told me that she got fired. I told her it was ok, she could get another job. I still didn't know what was going on. How could I not when I lived with it for most of my life? Well, it didn't take long after that to find out the truth. I got home after work and my boyfriend was pacing back and forth in the driveway. I got out of my car and asked him what was up. I had never seen him look so scared and worried. He told me to keep my mouth shut and to hear him out, that it was a matter of life and death. That's when a part of me died. He told me that one of our friends had called him up and said that Brooke was doing heroin and meth, and that she was totally out of control. He told me that her apartment was being watched and she was about to get busted. All I said was, "Take me to her apartment." When we got there, I walked in and told the two girls there to get out. Then Brooke came down the steps and told me to get out. I started screaming and yelling at her. Then I saw my cousin come down the steps, and I think I saw red. Brooke pushed me down a step and I just grabbed a hold of her and started beating her. I wanted to hurt her like I was hurting on the inside. She ended up pushing me out the door and told me to stay away.

By this time, Brooke was using and dealing, cooking up meth in her kitchen. A couple of days later, the cops raided Brooke's place. They found all sorts of paraphernalia and money, they took her phone, and dope of course. She had no idea where her car was and couldn't find her keys. We found out that some "friend" took her car and totaled it out on the grade road. I went to her place after work and she was just sitting there looking lost. She told me she wanted help but I didn't believe her. I told her she has my support and I have her back, but I wouldn't take her to detox. Some of her best friends since grade school took her to the hospital where she was admitted to the detox floor. She was in there for THREE days and then she went to a rehab. She was there for a couple days and called me and said to come get her, or she was "walking or calling a friend to come get her." I wasn't going to until my friend said, "do you really want her walking with all the nuts out there? Or having someone pick her up and they crash in the car?" So off we went to pick her up. That night, the cops set up a buy, and arrested Brooke. She called me from jail and I just went off on her, and she ended up saying she had to go. My father ended up putting his house up for bail. He picked her up at the jail and took her right to her apartment and she promised him she would go for help. After a whole day of procrastinating and getting high, a friend of mine who was taking her said she didn't know how Brooke didn't overdose, it was that bad. Off to detox she went, and then another rehab. This one was almost two hours away, however every Sunday my dad and I would truck up there for visiting hours. She almost made it her 90 days but left two days early because if she would've stayed, she wouldn't have been home for Christmas. That New Year's Eve, she got her first sponsor in the program. This girl didn't do much with her and ended up doing more harm than good. Brooke found another one. She was doing pretty good with her, but then the sponsor went back out!! Finally, the THIRD one was the Godsend who actually helped save Brooke's life. Brooke was doing really well, going to meetings every night, and working with her sponsor. They were inseparable for a while. Then Brooke ran into one of the girls she used to use with. It didn't take long for her to go back out with this girl. When one of your loved ones is an addict and they are in active use, especially a child, you barely sleep, eat, hell, function. Every time my phone would ring my heart would stop. It's like you are always fearing the worst. Well, it happened, my phone started to ring at 2:00 a.m. I thought, "Oh no, it's Brooke!" I looked at my phone and it was dad. This cannot be good. When I answered he was crying, and said that Brooke was in the Emergency Room. The doctors said she has to have brain surgery, and she is being flown to Altoona. I asked him what happened, and he said she wrecked her car. The people she was with called 911. So off to DuBois I flew. When I got into her room, I could tell she was high. Every question I asked her she would just laugh. I started to cry and she said, "Gee mom, you are more upset than I am." The doctor then came in to fill me in on details. He said, "Brooke was driving her car when she started to have a seizure. Thankfully there were two other people in the car. One of them grabbed the steering wheel and got the car off the road and then called 911. On the way to the hospital she had another seizure in the ambulance. Then she had her THIRD one right here in her room. Then he said he has never seen a 25-year-old girl with a brain that looked like hers.

He said one of his patients had a stroke, an older lady, and her brain even looked better than Brooke's! They were sending her to Altoona, just waiting for the paramedics to come and get her. I went out and asked the doctor if meth could do this to a person. He looked dumbfounded. That was something he didn't think he would hear.

I went home, got ready and off to Altoona I went along with my dad. On the way there, my pastor called me and asked me if it would be okay for him to meet me down there so he could go in and pray for her. I told him that would be wonderful. When he arrived, he was with another pastor, who is an Evangelist from Africa. All of us stood around Brooke's bed and the two pastors started to pray. Then my pastor stopped and let the other pastor pray. He prayed from the top of her head to the bottom of her feet. It was so beautiful! There just aren't any words that can express the faith that was in that room. You could tell the Lord was present. While he was finishing up they came to take Brooke to surgery, so we thought, but then the doctor came in and said she didn't need surgery, but they were going to do some tests and some other things. Those few hours seemed like an eternity! Finally, the doctor came out and started walking towards me. My heart stopped for that brief second. She came over and sat down beside me and said, "Your daughter ruptured some blood vessels in her brain. This is what caused the seizures and she was seconds away from having a stroke. I'm sorry to say but it is from the Meth. If she uses just one more time, it will kill her. Even if she gets hit in the head too hard it could kill her." She asked if I had any questions and I just shook my head. She told me when Brooke was ready to go back to her room someone would get me. My baby danced with the devil and got severely burnt.

When we got home, I was talking with her and she said she barely remembered anything from the accident on. She didn't remember the pastors praying either. I asked her if she remembers what the doctor told her. She said, "Yeah, yeah meth messed up my brain." I said, "Oh no, no, no, no, it is much worse than just that. The doctor said that if you get hit in the head hard enough it could kill you. And, and, and, if you ever, ever, EVER do meth again, it will kill you instantly! Do you understand that?" The look on Brooke's face at that moment in time, I will never forget.

Court day finally came, and of course I was scared to death. After sitting there for what seemed an eternity, Brooke finally got her sentence. The judge ended up giving her five years' probation, she lost her license for a year, and of course, there were fines.

A year went by and Brooke had an appointment with the doctor in Altoona. She asked me to go with her. I felt honored because we were starting to have the relationship that I always wanted.

Baby steps, that's all I asked for. When she got called into the room we heard these words that shocked the shit out of both of us. Not only did she have THREE seizures that night, she did have a stroke. Then she showed us a picture of her brain.

"MONSTERS ARE REAL AND THEY'RE TRAINED HOW TO KILL"

There are just no words I can say on how I felt at that moment in time.

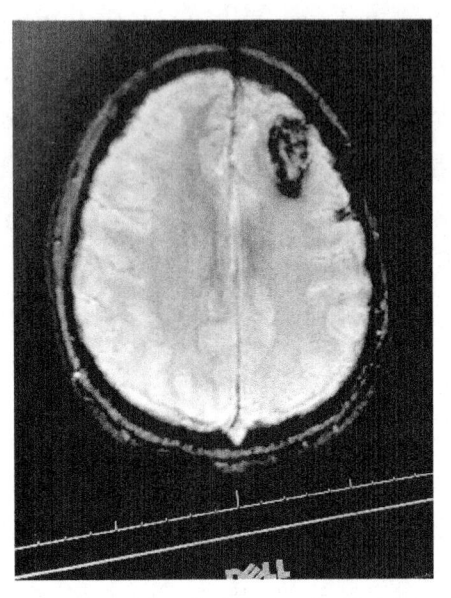

This is a picture of Brooke's brain after her injury and seizure. This is what Meth did to her brain.

After she started feeling better, Brooke went back to meetings and doing the 12 Steps with her sponsor. She was with her sponsor almost 24/7. I will never forget the day Brooke called me and said, "Hey mom, I am going to start taking classes to be a "Certified Recovery Specialist." She wanted to give back, like, paying it forward for all the help she received. She wanted to help other addicts just like the people who helped her. It was a six-week course and she wanted it so badly. And you know what? She did it!!! She got a job in no time, being a support person, and helping addicts wanting recovery to set goals! What a beautiful job! I am so beyond proud of her! She finally wanted out of hell so she kicked her demons' asses and sent them back to hell without her this time! They always will be circling around her, she just has to do things one day at a time.

She went from being a kid, to an addict who lost everything, overdosing THREE times, being arrested and put in jail, relapsing more than once, having seizures, a stroke, and part of her brain destroyed. Now she is the "fun & loving crazy Aunt", Godmother to two children, sponsor to others, and active in her meetings that helped save her life. She loves to go fishing and she adopted two dogs.

Now, why do I have the word "THREE" in all caps? Everything seemed to happen in threes and my belief is that this represents the Holy Trinity. "One God in three persons!" In this God we have Jesus Christ, who became one of us to take the punishment we deserved. In this God we have the person of the Holy Spirit, our Helper, and Divine Comforter, who lives in us to give us victory over sin. This triune God hears us when we pray, understands us when we suffer, and sees us safely home. (Adapted from Our Daily Bread Ministries)

Jesus said to the Christians, "that though their reputation had suffered some well-deserved hits, He had a new name reserved in heaven for those who fight back and conquer temptation. To the one who is victorious, I will give…a white stone with a new name written on it, known only to the one who receives it." (Revelation 2:17) Whatever the "white stone" may be, God promises our new name will wipe away our shame.

I know there is always a nightmare in the shadows lurking with demons and always breathing down your neck. When you feel the "breath of the demons" that should be the time you should stop and regroup, and get to a meeting, call your sponsor, or someone on the call list. You know deep down that a disaster is very near.

For Brooke everything started with trauma. She started with caffeine, cigarettes, alcohol, pills, pot, then meth and heroin. I know that she will never be "cured" from this disease, but just for today, she is sober and loving life. Her sobriety date is on my father's birthday. What better gift could there be than that? He had done so much for her and she thanked him with such an honor. I want to thank my dad for never giving up on her, the Rooms, my soul sisters Cece, and S.P. Without these THREE beautiful people, along with AA & NA, I know she wouldn't be here.

Just for today Brooke is sober by the grace of God. Tomorrow I will pray for her sobriety and thank the Lord if she is. Dr. Siar was right so many years ago. I have one tough daughter and nothing will keep her down! She never gave up the fight when she was born, and she doesn't give up the fight now. From the time she was born to the day my world ends, she is, and always will be, my warrior princess!!

In 2016, I filed for divorce for the THIRD time. Well the saying is true…Third time's the charm! And it was.

~ CyndiAnn AKA Symphony ~

If you want to learn more about addiction a good place to start in my opinion is:

"The Big book of Alcoholics Anonymous" the insight that is shared in this book are incredible. It has given me great comfort and knowledge.

Many things in this book touches my soul, but how "Bill W" says:

"No one can tell of the loneliness and despair I found in that bitter morass of self-pity. Quicksand stretched around me in all directions. I had met my match. I had been overwhelmed. Alcohol was my master."

— BILL W

"MS. ANNIE LEHMAN"

I was born and raised in Highland PA, where I spent the first six years of my life, with my mom, dad, and my autistic sister. We lived in a trailer on my papa's and grandma's property. My papa also had a junkyard where my dad worked. My mom was pretty busy caring for my autistic sister, and my dad was always working. When he wasn't working, he spent his spare time in a bar. I think it is safe to say now, that my father was an alcoholic. I was alone most of the time with the adults always being busy. So, I was very grateful for my papa. He would often take me for rides and we would visit the junkyard. I was always glad to go there because I would get to see my dad, even if it was only for a few minutes.

I would say, for the first six years, that I had a pretty normal childhood. I spent a lot of time with my cousin who taught me how to do cartwheels, make mud pies, ride bikes, and pick blueberries. I loved spending time with my cousin and Aunt. I am so glad I have that time in my life to reflect on. It taught me how to be a strong and independent woman. My papa uses to tell me that I could do anything that a man could do, and to never be afraid to use my voice, and never back down. Thankfully, my younger self held on, because those precious lessons eventually saved my life.

My mom and dad finally separated when I was six. My mom got pregnant with my little brother and after she had him, she met her husband and we moved to Ridgway. I barely got to see my father much after that, he ended up moving to Bradford, and never called or came to see me.

The move to Ridgway was when my life really took a turn for the worse. My mom started working a lot and her husband started hitting my sister. That is when I felt like I had to protect myself and my siblings from people who wanted to hurt us. We didn't have a lot of money and I always felt we were judged and made fun of. I started to hang out with older kids that hung out in the neighborhood. So, at seven years old, I started to run the streets. That is where I met my friend who was just as broken as I was. We had a special bond from that point on.

I started drinking at the age of seven with friends and family members. It started out that I would drink on holidays, but eventually grew into an everyday thing. I was sexually assaulted when I was younger and I believe it forced me to grow up faster than other girls my age.

I was bullied and made fun of in school, which was hard enough. Then they started to bully my disabled sister, and that is when I started fighting back. I remembered the lesson my papa taught me and I started using my voice! It was one thing to push me around, but now they were attacking my sister and I wasn't going to stand by and do nothing. Of course, that led to me being in the Principal's office, and spending a lot of time in the guidance counselor's office. I was angry, I was rebellious, and I felt, at times, it was me against the world. I resented anyone with authority. Why?

"MS. ANNIE LEHMAN"

Because none of them helped us. Life was so hard with all that was going on, and it seemed like nobody cared enough to do anything about it. I was the one always at fault; it wasn't the kids bullying me, it wasn't my stepdad who was hitting my siblings. I guess it was easier to blame me than for anyone else to take responsibility. This went on for years.

My mother was stuck in a toxic marriage, and I was out of control. At the age of ten, I got into a physical fight with my stepdad, I was tired of him hitting my siblings and I had enough. I again used my voice! I was sent to live with my father who I didn't even know anymore. That didn't work out well as his girlfriend couldn't handle us kids. If that wasn't bad enough, the one person I loved and who always made me feel loved and valued, my papa, died. My whole world seemed to fall apart. I remember that feeling so well; someone I loved was gone, and I didn't get to say goodbye.

Shortly after my eleventh birthday, we moved back with my mother. She had finally gotten out of her toxic marriage. I started dating an older boy, having sex, smoking weed, and snorting pills, all the while I was drinking regularly, and fighting. My mom had to start staying with friends when I started middle school. At twelve years old, my mom's friend's boyfriend sexually assaulted me, and I once again used my voice and spoke up. My mom and my siblings stayed at a friend's house and I stayed with other friends until mom could find us a place to live.

One morning I woke up to a female police officer there to drag me to school. I was so mad at that moment. What I didn't know at that time was that the female police officer and I were just starting a very long journey together. I also didn't know that she was going to play a huge part in saving my life.

After that, mom moved us back to Kane, and then moved us to Kersey. During that time, I was sexually assaulted again by a family member. This time I reported it. We went to court; however, the case was dismissed. His wife got on the stand and called me every name under the sun. She said I was lying because she was there the whole time and nothing happened. They asked me what I was wearing the day he assaulted me. I couldn't remember. Between that and her testimony, the case was dismissed. This had been the second time this man had assaulted me. The first time, I had kept quiet, as often children do. After all, who was going to believe me? I often wonder whether my problems didn't stem from his first assault. Yes, a lot of things factor into life choices, but a young woman having a grown-ass man force himself on you is something you just don't get over. It robs you, it takes something from you that you can't explain. It makes you not trust men, and in fact, anyone in an authority position. They didn't protect me! They didn't help me, so I was assaulted by him, and then raped by the system. Do you wonder why I had anger issues? Why I wanted to numb my pain? You are silenced in one way, so you want to make sure you are heard

"MS. ANNIE LEHMAN"

in other ways. Acting out and getting into trouble was my way of making people pay.

After that, I went to live with my dad, briefly. One day I came home after school and he informed me that he had received a call from Children and Youth Services, and that my baby brother was being placed in his custody, after being abused by the babysitter while my mom was working. I felt so guilty. I thought if I had been there, I could have protected him, and it would have never happened. I ended up moving back with my mother so I could be with my nonverbal little sister and keep an eye on her.

My mom met a guy and moved us off to Michigan, however that didn't last very long and we moved back to Ridgway.

I tried to kill myself for the first time after that. I was admitted to the psychiatric unit and started on my first round of psych meds. I had many interactions with the female police officer at this time. Skipping school, and out after curfew, I was a huge problem. I was angry and I was lashing out at everyone. The school decided that I needed to be put in a classroom away from the other students. That was when I met Mrs. O. I remember sitting there feeling so angry and this teacher seem to be able to feel my anger and pain. She came over and sat down and started talking to me. Not like the other teachers, she made me feel like she really cared about me. I was very open about my addiction problem, so everyone knew about it. Mrs. O. cared, she never judged me, and she always listened to me. Mrs. O. became the only person in the school that could handle me, I respected her and she truly cared about me. When I would start to act out in school, I would hear "Miss Annie Leman, you stop right there!" quite often.

At thirteen, I became an IV drug user, along with a group of other thirteen-year olds. The school had me going to drug and alcohol counseling on and off, from 7th to 8th grade. I had to go for a drug test, which I always passed because I kept clean urine on me all the time. I was always ready for those pop-up drug tests.

At the beginning of 8th grade, my dad showed up at my mom's house one morning, with my little brother. Because CYS was involved, my father had to inform them that he was residing with us for a while. My dad was kept in the dark about my active drug problem, my anger issues, and even my suicidal tendencies. When he found out, he was very angry at me, but also at himself. He realized that I was just like him, and even though he tried to buckle down with me, it wasn't working. 8th grade became a blur. I was trying all kinds of drugs; ecstasy, acid, and anything else I could. Yet, I kept passing the drug tests.

At the end of my 8th grade year, another student reported to Mrs. O. that I had cigarettes in my locker. She was forced to search my locker. The search resulted in her finding a pipe, knife, lighter, cigarettes, and empty pill bottle that I kept my clean urine in for my drug tests. The police were called and I was suspended until I could have a meeting with the superintendent. They gave me a drug test and this time I didn't pass it. I tested positive for THC, PCP, and cocaine. I had a meeting with the high school Principal, the middle school Principal, the Superintendent, and my parents. The high school Principal wanted to expel me, but my middle school Principal stuck up for me. They said that I was a pretty good kid who struggled with addiction, and that I needed help more than anything else. I was told that I had to go to rehab, or I wasn't allowed to come back to school.

That was my first time in rehab.

The weekend before I went to rehab, I reconnected with my older brother and sister. They had not been in my life much, so it was a little awkward for me in the beginning. Now I was going to spend the weekend with them. My older sister took me shopping for new clothes. I was really uncomfortable because this was the first time we had any real bonding and it was over me being a big disappointment to the family. Not only that, this was the first time in about six years that I had gone shopping for new clothes. My mom couldn't afford new clothes, often she could barely make ends meet.

I have always suffered from anxiety, and I believe a lot of it was because I lacked self-confidence. I always felt like I didn't belong anywhere. Maybe that is one of the reasons I felt comfortable being high. Anyway, I went to my first rehab at Clearbrook lodge in PA. I did 28 days. As I was sitting there I started telling myself I didn't belong there, that I didn't have a problem. I told myself, "I just smoked weed, and dabbled in other drugs." I didn't have a real problem, this was a mistake. I did my 28 days and came home. Of course, as part of my program, I had to attend meetings, I started to go to AA (Alcoholics Anonymous) because at the time there were no NA (Narcotics Anonymous) meetings close by. I only went to AA meetings a short time because I just felt uncomfortable going. I wasn't home for a month when I started doing things again; getting high and hanging out with my old group of friends. I was repeating my old pattern.

We all would hang out downtown at the basketball courts playing hacky sack. We had our favorite place, the "smoking tree," where we would meet up and smoke cigarettes or get high. That is where I ended up meeting the father of my children, I was 14, and we ended up together when I was 15. It seemed that we had this instant connection, we were both broken and we were both pretty much alone. We found comfort in each other's company, and we didn't feel alone anymore. It was a very codependent relationship, and at first, it was decent. But it wasn't long until it turned. I became toxic to him, and he became toxic to me. We started to experiment with harder drugs.

We stayed together and ended up getting married on April 14th, 2011. I was sixteen and on April 20th I found out that I was pregnant with my first child. Even though I was married now and pregnant, I was still under the care of CYS (Children and Youth Services) for not going to school and skipping school. I still had to answer them for my actions. They were taking me to court and wanted to put me into placement. There was a lot going and I was always arguing with the high school Principal. I was always so angry and fighting with everyone. I felt like everyone owed me something. I had a huge chip on my shoulder. Eventually, everyone got sick and tired of my shit. They had enough of my poor attitude. I was kicked out of school.

The Principal and the Superintendent made it clear that they did not want me in school anymore. CYS took me to court, where I was court-ordered into a "mom and baby" facility. I was also court ordered out of school. I was younger than the legal age to be signed out of school with parental consent. While I was in placement, I took classes to take my GED. Six months later, I turned 17, and I came home. I was eight months pregnant.

When I came home, I took my GED and passed. I realized that my husband at the time was pretty much down the "rabbit hole," and I had stayed sober and clean the whole time of my pregnancy. I was excited about becoming a mom and wanted all the things for my baby that I didn't have. I wanted the fairy tale life, the husband, children, and house; a whole family.

After I had my son, I started slowly getting back into drugs. First, I started smoking weed, but I didn't like it. It made it hard to take care of my baby. So, I ended up doing cocaine again. Then I went on Suboxone, and for a while, I only used Suboxone. However, it wasn't long before I started to use heroin and meth. I had tried them before I was pregnant, but it was different this time.

When my son was about two years old, my husband and I were in a really bad place. Our demons from the past started wreaking havoc on our marriage. Our drug addiction was out of control and became even more toxic than before. He became verbally abusive and I became physically abusive. It just wasn't healthy for either of us.

I was 18 now, and found out that I was pregnant with my second son. This was when bath salts made their debut in our area. We got extremely bad with bath salts. I ended up having an emergency C-section. After I had my son, I was still pretty bad into drugs. He was only a few months old when I ended up going to jail for a warrant. As I sat in jail, I had no choice but to get clean, which gave me time to reflect on what a shitty job I was doing. I was totally lost in my thoughts, and I had to acknowledge all the things that had been going on; what a bad mother I had become, the mean and rotten things I had said and all the things I had done. And, oh how bad I missed my children! I was overwhelmed with guilt and shame. I cried and cried, in fact, I cried a lot. I swore to myself that I would not go back and do it again.

The female police officer who had tried so hard to get me to go to school and to help me, was the one who arrested me. I spent a year in county jail, and I had other pending charges on me. One was for retail theft and the other was for selling bath salts. I had to do jail time for it as dealing bath salts was a pretty serious offense.

When I got out the first time, my ex went upstate and I realized how toxic we were for each other. Funny, the thing that brought us together was now the thing that was toxic in our relationship. I decided we had to go our separate ways.

I started to go to NA meetings after I got out of jail. I realized I had a problem and knew I needed help. However, I thought that drinking wasn't a problem, and that it didn't count. I mean, I didn't have a problem with alcohol. I could drink, and I would be fine. I figured I had put all the hard drugs down. Oh, how wrong I was. I learned the hard way. I became an alcoholic very quickly, I couldn't control myself, I always wanted more and I was making horrible decisions and I became somebody I didn't recognize. I ended up getting pregnant again, this time with a little girl. My morals were gone and I ended up back on the slippery slope of addiction.

After I had my daughter, I got really bad on painkillers again. I went to my probation officer and I told her I was in trouble, and I wanted to go to detox and rehab. I went to Maple Manor, where I learned a lot about myself. I spent 28 days there working the program. This time, I seemed to get more out of it. I really wanted to stay clean this time. I just wasn't sure how I would be able to do it.

Once I was released, I came home and walked into my apartment to find it completely trashed. My baby daddy was still using, my house was infested with bugs, and I had a total meltdown. I was trying so hard to get my life together for myself and my children, and it just seemed like it was one thing after another. Well, I broke, and I ended up admitting myself to the psych unit in Clarion.

I left the hospital and got a new place to live for the kids and me. It didn't take long after I was home to relapse, and I ended up back in jail. I was in jail for three days when my baby's dad took her, dropped her off at his sister's house, and never returned for her. I sat in county jail again for seven months, and then they sent me to a dual-diagnosed rehab for long-term rehab. It was the best rehab I had ever gone to: Conewago, in Snyder, PA. However, right before I went, I was served papers for emergency custody of my daughter. I was so hurt and angry, but there was nothing I could do. I had all these plans with my kids for when I got home.

I went to rehab and met the most amazing counselor. She helped me find my higher power, helped me find my spirituality, and she helped me understand why I was the way I was. I had gone to other rehabs and spent time in jail, but she helped me so much. I will say, that even though I relapsed many times and I failed, I would always pick myself up and try again. I never stopped learning about addiction. I never stopped learning about myself and what makes me tick.

After I got out of rehab, I came home to the same thing. They tell us to change people, places, and things. I didn't do any of them. I once again relapsed, and I was on the run. I was running from parole, and I was running from my family. I decided I would detox myself and get clean, come home, turn myself in, and go back to rehab.

However, I got a phone call. My grandmother was in bad shape and wasn't going to make it. I needed to come home. We all met up at the nursing home in Kane, PA, and I said my goodbyes. I decided to stay in Elk county.

This was not a good idea. I got so bad. I was doing so much meth and heroin. I am surprised that I am even here to tell my story. I was way past the point of caring. I tried to talk to my kids, but the people who had them refused to let me even talk to them on the phone because I was such a mess. I was afraid I would never have the chance to be the mom I so desperately wanted to be. I loved my kids, that is the thing that people don't understand. Being an addict didn't make me unable to love. Of course, I loved them with all my heart. But I was stuck in this world of addiction that I knew so well. It was something I had been doing for a long time. I lost hope of ever having my children back again. With losing that hope, I lost hope in myself, I didn't care if I lived or died. I was in a very dark place. In the mornings, I would wake up feeling so dope sick that I would just lay there and cry, I was so tired of it. I was tired of getting high, I was tired of living my life this way. I was tired of feeling like a failure. I was tired of not being there for my children.

On my last Christmas, I was home, and I was on the run. I was at my mom's house. I missed my kids so much. As I was standing in her kitchen I promised myself that I would get my life together so I could get my kids back and celebrate Christmas with them.

I knew it was a matter of time until I was arrested on one of my warrants, so shortly after Christmas, I was arrested in the Smethport hotel. I was sent to the McKean County jail, and then Elk County came and got me. I ended up sitting there for a while, I wrote a letter to the DA and to the Judge and asked if they would send me to State prison. I had heard there were many programs that I could benefit from.

I was sentenced to Muncy State Prison for 2 ½ to 5 years. In Muncy, I took multiple classes and was involved in groups. I think the state program therapeutic groups were the best things I was involved with. I went into a living safely for women group. it taught me about my worth. I did everything I was supposed to do. I spent time talking to other women there who were in for life because of drug addiction and murder. They shared the best advice and stories with me. I learned so many things from them

When I got a chance to call home, I would tell my kids that I was going to do my best to stay clean and be a good mom. I had learned not to promise them, even though I wanted to stay clean and be everything I could be, I had broken enough promises, and I wasn't making anymore. It wasn't because I didn't want to stay clean. I did! I just would find myself back into that vicious cycle until I would think I had hit rock bottom. I learned you don't hit your rock bottom until you stop digging.

While I was in state prison, I got served with papers to terminate my parental rights to my daughter. I had to make a choice, so at the court hearing, I had to weigh out my options. I knew I had been very selfish during my addiction; I was even more selfish with my children. I had to think about what was best for all of them. My daughter was born with a disability with her eyesight. She had been living with her Aunt and Uncle her entire life. She never knew me because I wasn't around. I was in and out of jail most of the time. She was happy, and they truly loved her, and she loved them. They both could do more for her and provide her with the life I could not. As much as I wish things were different, they weren't, and the best decision was the right one. I signed over my rights to them and let them adopt her. They send me photos and let me know how she is doing.

However, my boys knew me and had lived with me. I was in their lives more. I had to focus on them and my children's father. I had done so much damage to our relationship, and I had to figure out how to make things right. It's hard now to think about what I did to my beautiful children. It will haunt me until the day I die.

I came home from prison in January of 2020, I have been clean and sober, and I work really hard. I am involved in NA (Narcotics Anonymous), but best of all, I have full custody of my boys now. They live with me, and I work really hard. I know a lot of people doubted me. I have to say, I was scared, also. But I would go to meetings, come home and be a mom. I refused to hang out with anybody.

Two weeks after I got out of prison, my ex came around. He was still battling his addiction. I ended up having to resuscitate him from and overdose. It was so scary. I felt like I had to save him, but it almost cost me my sobriety. He ended up going to jail, which probably saved his life, and I am very thankful that it did.

I kept attending meetings and worked on repairing my relationship with my boys. My son endured a lot trauma. One day he exploded on me and let me have it, telling me how I had hurt him repeatedly. I could see the anger on his face. Most of all, I could see the pain in his eyes. It was hard standing and letting him vent on me, but he was right, and I had to suck it up. He was right, and I had let him down time and time again.

My goal was to stay sober and to work on life for my kids and me. I had to learn how to be a single mom. I had no idea how to go about this because I was so young when I started using. I knew I needed to find a job and a place for us to live. And that wasn't easy. My name was well known.

I met my future husband; he has been an amazing person. I celebrated Christmas with my children and my fiancé and with my father for the first time in a long time. In one short year, I worked hard and accomplished all my goals. We both have jobs and work hard together. The kids have an amazing role model in their lives now, also.

Unfortunately, that year, I also experienced a great loss. I got a phone call that they were taking my dad to the hospital. He was confused, and something was wrong. I rushed over to the hospital to be with him. I was told he had cancer and it had spread all through his body, and he was terminal. Understand, my dad was my biggest supporter. He would always do whatever he could to encourage me and help me even when I was at my lowest. He never gave up hope on me. When I was in jail, he never missed a visit. He would always yell at me when I did wrong. All the guilt returned to me. It crushed my world, and I lost all that time with him. I only had one year with him. My dad passed away. All the years in and out of jail and being high. I lost all my valuable time with him.

Not even one month after my father passed, I got a phone call that my childhood best friend had died. She was supposed to be my bridesmaid at my wedding. It was too much, and I started to make bad decisions. I started hanging around people that I shouldn't be around, and I knew it. I ended up taking a hit of weed. Many people think that weed doesn't hurt your sobriety, but that isn't the case with me. I know that I have to stay away from all drugs and alcohol. So, I took responsibility for what I did. I called my sponsor from NA, I called my family and I confessed to what I did.

I knew if I gave into it, I would be going down that slippery road, and it wouldn't take long and I would be right back where I started from, and I didn't want that.

I have a nice home, a wonderful man in my life, my boys live with me, and life is good. It is what I have always wanted.

I finally realized what was taking me backwards. It was all the past trauma and pain that I had suffered from. I used it as an excuse to get high, it was so easy to play that victim card. I always felt I had to take things I needed, that I was never good enough. I realize that normal life has pain, and you must learn to work through the pain.

In rehab and other therapeutic communities (prison), I learned how to work on my trauma, my PTSD, and my abuse. It was where I needed to be to learn the lessons I needed to learn. Yes, some days are harder than others, especially when you experience loss and grief. I don't even think at all about doing meth or heroin. I don't need it in my life. It isn't what I want at all.

My goal is to help as many young people as I can reach. I remember when I was younger and felt so alone. I didn't know that my life wasn't normal, and many young kids live that life. They don't know that there is another life or any way out. They think it is normal because that is their life. To be honest, many young people don't trust people in authority because they have been let down by them or judged. So many of us hide all the crap going on, even when we know it isn't right. We hide it because of shame and guilt. I was beaten down badly when I was a kid, I always felt inadequate, and everything I did was wrong. After you hear it so much, you believe it.

I don't take my recovery for granted, it is life long battle, and I know it. I fight for today, one second, one minute and one day at a time. I will continue to go to meetings and I will continue to do my best. Thank you to all my family and friends who never gave up on me. To all of you that made me understand that I am worth so much more.

~**Annie**

PART III

Addiction touches so many lives.
When we think about it, we think about how it effects the families. But it has a "ripple" effect throughout
the community. It touches and changes everyone it comes into contact with.
These are stories from people who have a different view on Substance Use Disorder. They have seen it up close and personal, also. It has touched their lives and has forever changed them.
Thank you, my dear friends, for helping us all to understand and for sharing your voice.

FROM ADDICT TO ADDICTION PROFESSIONAL

~BY CHELSEY STAUFFER~

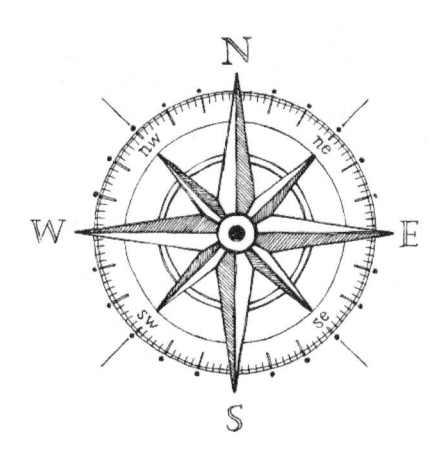

My name is Chelsey, and I am a grateful recovering addict. When I was new, I hated when "old timers" said that. Why on earth would anyone be grateful to be an addict? Now I understand. Today words cannot describe how grateful that I am to be an addict. If I never became addicted to drugs, I wouldn't have the life I have today. Because I found recovery, I now feel as if I have a purpose on this planet. My experiences in active addiction laid the groundwork for the direction that my life would take. Despite the despair, agony, and fear, I wouldn't change a moment of it. The trials and tribulations that I endured during those years, taught me invaluable lessons that I wouldn't trade for the world. Of course, there are things that I have done that I will regret for the rest of my life- most importantly hurting the people I love the most- but that's not the person I am anymore. I plan to spend the rest of my life making up for the hurt that I have caused.

My father died when I was 8 years old. I was always a "daddy's girl", and suddenly I was left to adjust to life without him. My 8-year-old brain didn't know how to comprehend such a devastating loss, so I began to develop unhealthy coping skills. I created fantasy worlds where I would play pretend for days on end so that I didn't have to be me. I would escape into these worlds so that I didn't have to be Chelsey. I didn't have to feel the way Chelsey did. I learned that talking about my feelings was hard and painful, so I chose to bottle it up and ignore the pain. My mom tried taking me to therapists and psychologists, but I was not having it. Thank God for my mom. She always had my back- it just took me a while to realize it.

Fast forward a few years, and my "coping skills", became more troublesome. I began self-harming, which I now know was its own addiction. I threw myself into schoolwork and started obsessing over grades. I spent hours upon hours every night studying, escaping from my own reality again. Then in high school, my eldest brother was diagnosed with cancer. Not long after, he passed away. At this point I had started hanging around a new group of kids, and senior year I began drinking and smoking pot. School was less important to me now. All I wanted to do was party and get high. Parties and drugs became my new favorite escape. If I was high, I wasn't in pain. If I was at parties, I wasn't home to see the hurt in my mother's eyes.

The next couple of years were a blur. Shortly after cancer took my brother's life, my mother was diagnosed with cancer. The thought of possibly losing my mother next was too much to bear, so I ran... and I ran hard. Party drugs were no longer doing the trick. I graduated to heroin, bath salts, and meth. I began using needles. I lied, I manipulated, I stole, and I cheated to keep the high going. I wasn't there for my mom when she needed me the most. I was selfish and self-seeking, but mostly I was afraid.

There is however a happy ending to this story. My mom went into remission, and because she always believed in me and never gave up on me- I stayed alive. If it wasn't for my mom's support through the psych ward, treatment centers, emergency rooms, doctors, and relapses, I probably would have killed myself. But I couldn't kill myself; I wasn't going to let my mom mourn the death of another child. I was facing criminal charges for stealing from my former place of employment and facing eviction in an apartment with no heat. My apartment was just robbed by so called "friends"- they even took my phone. I was dope sick. I was in and out of psychosis and was highly unstable, but my mom was fearless. She came into my apartment to attempt an intervention. About a week later I conceded. After years of running, I found myself back in another treatment center- beaten and broken.

Something was different this time. To this day, I'm not sure what it was, but this time I was ready to do whatever it took. I wanted a new life. I was tired of living the way I was living. So, I turned my life over the treatment professionals, and I took all their suggestions. After inpatient, I followed direction and went into long term care and a sober living house. I went through the entire continuum of care (I'll explain what this is later) and built a brand-new life for myself across the state. Sometimes I miss Elk County, but I have something special here in the Poconos. Something that I don't feel like I need to escape from. My mom once told me that I am more of a daughter to her now living 5 hours away than I was when I lived 15 minutes down the road. Repairing the relationship with my mom has been the single greatest gift that recovery has ever given me. I am beyond grateful for everything she has done for me.

My clean date is February 20, 2018. My recovery is an abstinence-based program. I am free from all mind or mood-altering substances. I sometimes wonder if I could drink or smoke pot like a "normal" person now that I have been removed from active addiction for a while. However, I do know that it is highly unlikely that I could drink without the inevitable unmanageability that comes with it. It's a gamble and I am *not* willing to gamble with my life today. So, I choose not that take that risk, because I am still terrified of the hell that is active addiction. Therefore, I continue to participate in a 12-step program, I continue to work with a sponsor, I help the newcomers, and I continue to grow spiritually enjoying living life to its fullest. Because of recovery, I am no longer that scared, sad little girl looking to escape. I am a fiancé, employee, student, friend, and daughter and I want to be present for every second of it.

The people who worked in those treatment centers were so influential to me in early recovery. They showered, brushed their teeth, and went to work every day. Things that I was completely incapable of doing at that point. But even more remarkably, they were sober and happy. They had families and hobbies. They were kind and patient. They gave me hope that I could live a life worth living in recovery. I wanted that. I wanted to do what they did. I wanted to be able to be the hope for the next scared little girl who walked into detox. For the first time in my life, I had an inkling of what my future could look like. I feel forever indebted to the professionals that helped pull me out of the gutter. They gave me permission to talk about how I was feeling and helped me to realize that feelings won't kill me; that it was healthy to have emotions. These were all concepts that felt so foreign to me. They walked with me through the emotional rollercoaster that is early recovery and helped me rediscover myself. It was like I was meeting a complete stranger; I had to relearn who Chelsey is.

At a year and a half clean, I got my first job working in treatment as a behavioral health technician. It was my first real full-time job with benefits, and I was so excited. I was going to help others like others helped me. I found how I can turn my ugly past into something beautiful. Since my career began, I have had the privilege to work in a plethora of different positions- Client Care Coordinator, Case Manager, Lead Case Manager, and Supervisor of Care Operations. I will never forget the first patient that was assigned to my case load or my first office. It still blows my mind how far I have come, and how amazing recovery is.

Now I work in Marketing and Outreach at a 30-day premier residential treatment facility in Scotrun, PA. My current position affords me the ability to travel and meet people from all over. I get to tell them all about the wonderful things that happen in our program and spread the word about us so that more people can get the help they need. I also have the privilege of getting to meet industry professionals from across the county. I help people get into treatment and try to save lives every day. Even if it's not with us, I help addicts like me get the help that they deserve. It's incredibly rewarding, and I love every minute of it.

I want to preface this by saying that I am by no means an expert. I am not a licensed clinician (working on it) and I am not a medical provider. I am just an addict who has been working in addiction treatment for a number of years. I almost turned down this opportunity to write from an "addiction professional's" point of view, because my low self-esteem wouldn't allow me to consider myself within that category. However, a woman in Executive Leadership encouraged me to write this reassuring me that I am qualified and that I do have experience to share. Through these years, I have gained extensive knowledge and experience about the kinds of help that is available to those with substance use disorders. I have seen so many success stories, and I believe in the work that is being done by the experts in my field. I do know that help is available, and recovery is possible. I've seen it with my own eyes, so I have been asked to share some of my knowledge on how substance abuse disorders are treated and how one can find help.

Addicts and alcoholics today are far more fortunate today than ever before. More beautiful rehab programs are cropping up every day making accessibility to treatment easier than ever. I want to be clear here; treatment centers don't have a "cure". There is no secret formula to dispel the disease of addiction. These programs don't work for those who *want* to get better. They work for those who do the work it takes to get better. If wanting to get clean was enough; I would have gotten clean ages ago. It doesn't work until you are ready to make some sacrifices and do things differently.

I mentioned the full continuum of care before, and how I was in long term treatment. It can take eight years or more to achieve long-term remission from substance use disorders regardless of the treatment avenue taken.1 So from my own personal experience and from what I have seen after years of working in addiction treatment, the longer one stays in treatment; the better. Healing the brain and body after addiction takes time, which is why the continuum of care was developed. A full continuum of care includes medically managed detox, residential, partial hospitalization, intensive outpatient, and outpatient services. It is designed to be a step-down process that slowly tapers patients down into lower levels of care. It slowly integrates patients back into society while still being under clinical supervision to help ensure a smooth transition into normal daily life. Eight years is a long time, and I don't know anyone who has been in treatment for 8 years. However, if one follows the full continuum, they have a good foundation onto which they can continue to build. Most insurances will cover a full continuum if it is deemed medically and clinically appropriate.

- 1 Brian Mann, "There is Life After Addiction. Most People Recover", *Most people with alcohol and drug addiction survive: NPR*, January 15, 2022; https:www.npr.org/2022/01/15/1071282194/addiction-substance-recovery-treatment, (accessed December 13, 2022).

The length and duration of treatment necessary varies from person to person based on the ASAM criteria. The ASAM criteria is a set of guidelines based on patient assessments that examine six dimensions of a person's particular circumstances. These dimensions include past and current substance use, health history and physical needs, mental health and cognitive function, readiness to change, risk for relapse, and living conditions.2 Addiction professionals who provide these assessments use the ASAM criteria to place patients into the most appropriate level of care for the best outcomes and to facilitate referrals to appropriate providers. These assessments can be provided by most licensed clinicians and can even be completed at your county's Drug and Alcohol office. The Drug and Alcohol office can also provide resources to those who are uninsured or underinsured.

- 2 "About the ASAM Criteria", *About the ASAM Criteria,* American Society of Addiction Medicine, 2022, http://www.asam.org/asam-criteria/about-the-asam-criteria, (accessed December 13, 2022). 3 "Key Substance Use and Mental Health Indicators in the United States: Results from the 2020 National Survey on Drug Use and Health", *Substance Abuse and Mental Health Services Administration,* October 2021, https://www.samhsa.gov/data/sites/default/files/

reports/rpt35325/
NSDUHFFRPDFWHTMLFiles2020/
2020NSDUHFFR1PDFW102121.pdf, (accessed
December 14, 2022).

It's no secret that substance abuse and mental health disorders often go hand in hand. In fact, in 2020 there were 17 million adults in the US that suffer from both SUD and co-occurring mental health diagnoses.3 I've seen the acuity of mental health disorders among SUD patients skyrocket over the past couple years. I'm not sure why this is happening, but it is undeniable that people are generally sicker now for whatever reason. To help offset the rise in mental health concerns, many substance abuse treatment programs are now co-occurring or dual- diagnosis. Many also offer genetic testing. These tests analyze patients' genetic makeup to determine which medications will metabolize best in their bodies. This testing can help to take the guess work out of medication management to allow patients to stabilize on a medication that will work for them quicker than ever before. I've seen the benefits of such testing and its remarkable the difference that the correct medication can make.

Many options for MAT are available for patients that are appropriate. Not everyone is appropriate for these medications as some of them can be habit forming, but I have seen them work wonders when they are used properly, managed by a medical addiction professional, and coupled with substance abuse counseling. MAT medications are medications used to help mitigate some of the cravings associated with early recovery. Common MAT medications are Naltrexone, Vivitrol, Suboxone, and Sublocade. Naltrexone is a daily pill that is most often used for alcohol and opioid use disorders. Vivitrol is a once a month extended-release injection used for alcohol and opioid use disorders. Suboxone is an oral medication, often sublingual, that is used to treat opiate addiction and can be used for pain management. Sublocade is a once-a-month injection that contains the same medication as Suboxone used to treat moderate to severe opioid use disorders. Most treatment programs have medical professionals on staff that can evaluate patients to see if they are a candidate for these medications.

Therapy is a paramount component to substance use treatment. I have seen talented clinicians completely change the trajectory of people's lives. There are many common treatment modalities that are commonly seen in treatment programs. Some of these therapies are Cognitive Behavioral Therapy, Dialectal Behavior Therapy, Rational Emotive Behavior Therapy, and Motivational Interviewing. These therapies can be done at an inpatient or outpatient level. EMDR has also become more common for treating trauma in those who suffer from substance use disorders. EMDR stands for Eye Movement Desensitization and Reprocessing. It is a type of therapy that allows patients to work through their trauma while simultaneously experiencing bilateral stimulation to change the way that memories are stored in the brain.4 At my current place of employment, the clinical work is the life blood of the program. We could not provide the quality treatment that we do without the world class therapists that work with our patients. It is so integral to the success of persons who suffer with addiction.

- 4 "Eye Movement Desensitization and Reprocessing (EMDR) Therapy", *Eye Movement Desensitization and Reprocessing (EMDR) Therapy (apa.org)*, 2022 American Psychological Association, May 2017, https://www.apa.org/ptsd-guidelines/treatments/eye-movement-reprocessing, (accessed December 13, 2022)
- 5 "Key Substance Use and Mental Health Indicators in the United States: Results from the 2020 National Survey on Drug Use and Health", *Substance Abuse and Mental Health Services Administration*, October 2021, https://www.samhsa.gov/data/sites/default/files/reports/rpt35325/NSDUHFFRPDFWHTMLFiles2020/2020NSDUHFFR1PDFW102121.pdf, (accessed December 14, 2022).

In recent years, the COVID-19 pandemic has caused treatment providers to rethink the way that substance use treatment is provided. I think this is worth mentioning because I personally think that this is super exciting as it opens opportunities for more people to get help. Of all the people aged 12 or older who received substance use treatment in Quarter

4 of 2020, fifty-eight percent reported receiving virtual or telehealth services.5 Due to the demand for these types of services, insurance companies began expanding reimbursements for persons receiving these types of services making it easier to seek help virtually. In my opinion, in person services tend to be more effective but SAMSHA has reported that virtual services have been showing positive results. These services make treatment more accessible for those who live in rural areas, which is a great step in the right direction in improving accessibility across the country.

I would be amiss if I didn't mention the tried-and-true self help support groups such as Alcoholics Anonymous and Narcotics Anonymous. These programs have been used for decades in treating alcoholism and addiction. I'm a 12-step gal myself. Treatment centers still introduce these programs to patients, but now other options for support groups have been gaining popularity. For people who struggle to relate in 12-step programs, other avenues are being presented as alternative options to the traditional 12 step model. Some of the more popular groups are SMART Recovery and Dharma Recovery. SMART Recovery stands for Self-Management and Recovery Training. It is a support group led by volunteers that utilizes science based cognitive therapy tools to help people self-manage their negative thinking patterns. Dharma Recovery is a non-theistic path to addiction recovery that teaches Buddhist skills and principles to encourage and sustain sobriety. What's neat is that all these programs are more accessible now than ever before. The pandemic has forced many groups to explore virtual meeting spaces which has made it so much easier to attend the program of your choice. Virtual meetings can be found online 24/7. The impact of the ease of access cannot be understated. Anyone can attend free online meetings at any time. Recovery is about getting uncomfortable and requires sacrifices. It requires one to do things that they don't want to do and trust people who have experience. When people take a chance and follow suggestions, miracles happen. I have seen young kids build lives for themselves and get married. I have seen families reunite. I have seen people come into treatment in a wheelchair gain their strength back and regain mobility. I have seen people come in with yellow skin from jaundice get their color back. I have seen the most anxious and depressed patient turn a corner and become a community leader. I know people in recovery that are now attorneys, business owners, policemen, mothers, and politicians. That addict stealing from Walmart isn't a bad person, just a sick person. The mother who lost her children didn't choose drugs over her kids. Addiction isn't a moral problem; it's a disease that makes good people do bad things and make bad choices. However, the disease can be arrested.

The first step to getting help is to ask for help. Insurance companies can point you in the direction of programs that they cover. If you are uninsured, your county Drug and Alcohol office can help to find funding. Go online, do your research, ask a professional, or go to a meeting. One thing that I know for certain is that we can't fight this disease alone. Help is available and recovery is possible. SAMHSA's National Helpline phone number is 1-800-662-4357. It's confidential and available 24/7. They also have an online treatment locator. AA.org and NA.org have search engines to help locate meetings near you. Psychology Today is a great resource for finding clinicians and treatment providers. If you or a loved one is struggling with the disease of addiction, my phone is always on- (570) 534-7326.

LEADING THROUGH ADVERSITY

PREPARED BY: W. TODD CATALGARONE
SHERIFF OF ELK COUNTY

Leading Through Adversity

Unless one experiences the senseless and unexpected death of a close family member because of an accidental drug overdose, it is very difficult to fully empathize with that loss. It has been described by parents who lose a child in this manner as a feeling of helplessness. Elk County confronts the problem of unlawful use of drugs through education, treatment, recovery, enforcement, investigation, prosecution, diversion, and eradication. Yet, the problem remains. However, with the availability of the opioid reversal drug Narcan (Naloxone) now widely available, and with law enforcement and other first responders who are trained and equipped to administer that medication, many lives have been saved with their immediate response and use of Narcan to reverse the effects of an opioid overdose. Still, much more needs to be done. Law enforcement organizations are steeped in tradition, rules, regulations, systems, and processes, and are naturally resistant to change. Nevertheless, they have proved the ability to adapt over time in order to meet the present challenges with the resources at hand. We are faced with a problem that is complex and dangerous with a deep and winding root system that requires deeper cooperation and collaboration. It began many years ago in small towns in Appalachia, with abuse of prescription opioid medications, and has progressed to injectable heroin and fentanyl. As such, law enforcement and the justice system are now working closer than ever, and together with programs like LETA (Law Enforcement Treatment Initiative), to identify qualified persons at various levels of use, and divert or direct them to treatment and recovery centers in lieu of the criminal justice system. Medical Assisted Treatment (MAT) has also shown positive results, especially with the use of Vivitrol, a very expensive injectable medication.

Although the abuse of opioids is most concerning because of the immediate effect that can result in breathing cessation and death, there are many other dangerous drugs that are abused that negatively impact and disrupt the social strata of society, and that interrupt family, workforce, education, healthcare, culture, and other life domains. Methamphetamines, for one, have been on the rise and found to be used in conjunction with other drugs. Unlawful drug abuse leads to Substance Use Disorder and respects no geographical borders, socio-economic groups, and has no prejudices. With the rural nature of Elk County, we find ourselves struggling with transportation and access issues, even as access is improving tremendously. The flip side of that is convincing the drug user in need to accept treatment and recovery when it is offered to them. The majority of time after reversing the results of an opioid overdose by administering the life-saving drug Narcan, the victim refuses transport to a medical facility and follow-up treatment. That is another rub to the problem.

It is also important to be mindful of the fact that Narcan is available for purchase at any pharmacy via a protocol prescription made available to them by the Pennsylvania's Physician General. That makes it is difficult to posit how many lives have been saved that go unreported.

To provide the readers with what happens on the initial end of a reported witnessed overdose with breathing cessation here is what occurs. It begins with a 911 call being placed to the Elk County Office of Emergency Services. A quick intake is conducted using the CAD (Computer Aided Dispatch) system where the call is given a specific priority level. In this case both EMS (Emergency Medical Services) and law enforcement would be signaled for a drug overdose with breathing cessation, followed by some specific details obtained through the 911 Center Intake, with a priority level of "Echo." In a nutshell an "Echo" level event indicates a life threating situation and takes priority over all others. In most cases, law enforcement is the first to arrive on scene and after an immediate assessment administers Narcan via a spray into the nasal cavity. Where necessary CPR (Cardio Pulmonary Resuscitation) is applied and/or an AED (Automated External Defibrillator) utilized. Those life saving measures are performed, usually resulting in a reversal and restoration of breathing. The victim, who is now a patient, is transferred to EMS personnel. On occasion, when those efforts fail due to any number of reasons, the Coroner is summoned to the scene to pronounce the person deceased, and a joint investigation between the Coroner's Office and law enforcement is commenced.

However, death by accidental overdose is not the only way that use of unlawful drugs kill. I will share one example. Many years ago, I recall an incident where emergency services signaled first responders during the early morning hours for a vehicle crash. Upon arrival many of the first responders discovered that they knew the driver of the vehicle that had crashed. The young man had crossed the oncoming lane on the roadway and crashed head on into a tree. Rescue technicians went to work to extricate the driver. The driver's father arrived on scene. I recall his words that morning. He said, "That's my son" before he collapsed to the ground on his knees and remained that way with a catatonic look on his face throughout the entire rescue operation. The vehicle sustained major crush damage and the driver was seriously entrapped and entangled inside the vehicle. It took several minutes for first responders to spread and cut away parts of the vehicle to reach the driver. He was obviously deceased having suffered severe chest and head trauma.

The young driver was transported to the hospital emergency room where he was cleaned of blood and debris before his parents viewed him. His mother fell over his lifeless body repeatedly calling his name while wailing uncontrollably. Her dead son was only 18 years old. The subsequent investigation revealed that he was under the influence of an unlawful drug. The tree that the young driver crashed into still stands today. He was only two blocks from his home. That incident occurred many years ago, yet I still recall the vivid details. The anguish and absolute helpless feeling that parents experience when they lose a son or daughter is palpable, and one of the very worst events to experience and live through.

Law enforcement, the criminal justice system, members of the community, other interested groups both public and private sector related, and social services are all committed and dedicated to the preservation of life and to enhancing the health and safety of their communities. It requires good collaboration that also includes educational systems, faith-based institutions, and various non-profits all coming together with strategies that follow a multi-dimensional approach with the objectives of enhancing health and safety and neutralizing motivations and the means to offend that results in destructive and life-threatening behavior. Why should we do this? Perhaps many of you heard the tale as it relates to the "Starfish Story." I am not sure who to give credit for the story as there are so many versions, but is goes something like this:

A young woman was walking along a beach where hundreds of starfish has been washed up from the giant waves. As she came to each starfish she would pick it up and toss it back into the waves. A man approached her and asked her what she was doing. She replied that she was throwing the stranded starfish back into the ocean so that they can live. The man replied that she can't possibly make a difference in that the beach was miles long and there were hundreds if not thousands of starfish. He asked her if she really thought what she was doing could make a difference. The young woman paused, picked up a starfish and tossed it back into the ocean and said, "It makes a difference for that one."

The moral of the starfish story is that every life is important and when faced with impossible odds it demands an ongoing commitment to do your very best, and to do whatever you can to make a difference in terms of the well-being of the individual. We are not going to save everyone, but we can and will work to problem solve and save as many as we can. It will continue to take leaders who can lead transformation and change and who are people centered; leaders who will work to collect, analyze, process, fuse and disseminate information in a timely manner; leaders who are enthusiastic, self-motivated, realistic and who are concerned with solving problems (Ratcliffe, 2003); leaders who know how to gain commitment and organize people around a shared vision, and who can focus and synergize efforts toward a common objective; leaders with the compassion to listen to the needs of others; finally, leaders who, by the quality of their actions and the integrity of their intent, are authentic with core values of trust and empathy, and who are willing to be at the center of any effort. This all distills down to transformational leadership. Doing more with less, but doing it better and faster, is the challenge of transformational leadership (Warrick, 2011). In this era of continuous uncertainty, faced with a new type of threat, a proactive approach is in order to thrive and succeed. Properly employed, the right kind of leadership builds trust and unites people around common goals thereby creating a higher order of thinking in developing effective strategies. These are leaders who can clearly communicate what needs to be done, how it should be done and why it needs to be done. This fundamental skill rallies stakeholders and keeps them united and focused. Information and the capacity to communicate are critical in the new information age. Maxwell (2006) emphasized that consistency and predictability breeds trust. Also important are pure motives and strong character as fundamental tenets in getting the backing and support of communities in working the problem of drug abuse and Substance Use Disorder. Citizens are primary stakeholders and as such have an essential role in keeping their neighborhoods and communities safe. An emotionally intelligent response to people's concerns and issues whether real or perceived is another essential factor.

The problem with the abuse of unlawful drugs has been a long time in the making and will take time to work through. It is appropriate to view the problem in a broader context in terms of truly understanding the depth of the problem and the long-term commitment that it will take in confronting it. There are many issues that accelerate the problem through indirect means such as technology. Technology has increased our awareness of the problem, but it has also exacerbated it. The acceleration through technology tends to shorten the time frame from working a specific issue in terms of getting into a decision loop and transacting a response. However, there is hope. Although there are some things out of our control, there are many things within our control. More recently the multi-faceted and comprehensive strategies and greater cooperation and collaboration between private and public sector agencies has improved greatly. Awareness has been heightened and many lives have been saved through awareness, education, treatment services, recovery services, and the availability of Narcan, and where necessary, investigation, arrest, and prosecution. The work that is being done every day aims to protect our communities, neighborhoods and families while working to address the needs of people in crisis. Progress is being made. We can never give up.

Lt. General Hal Moore, an American hero and a great example of a leader is quoted as saying, "Lead where the action is." He is remembered for his military leadership, especially when he led his battalion into combat against the People's Army of Vietnam in IA Drang, which was the first direct military engagement in Vietnam. Among his leadership principles he is quoted as saying, "That there is always one more thing you can do to influence a situation in your favor to increase your odds of success. Think of what else it is that you can do. The more things you can do opens opportunities." He reminds us that life will bring with it adversities, but to prevail we have to believe in ourselves. Collins (2001) refers to the Hedgehog Concept as fundamental and central to greatness. The Hedgehog is committed to its purpose, never wavering and moves continuous and steady towards his objective. It consists of three dimensions: what a person is passionate about, what a person can be best at and what drives a person's engine. Tenets such as competence, empowerment, vision, trust, trustworthiness and caring follow this strategy. Covey (2003) posited that whatever is at a person center is what will drive him or her. He espoused a true north principle centered leadership that is rooted in mutual respect, honor and trust that is naturally reciprocal.

With that we know, the risk of repeat overdose is significant in that it is chronic among those in need of Substance Use Disorder Treatment. We understand more how the effects of Substance Use and Misuse effects brain chemistry and the neurobiology of the brain through advances in scientific research. Therefore, the path to treatment and recovery is long and must be sustainable (https://addiction.surgeon general.gov). It will take much more than the criminal justice-based model, which communities tend to rely on. The problem has many legs and is also in need of strategies that are more holistic in terms of addressing the social, economic, and environmental factors that go directly to the health and safety of communities.

The real test of class and leadership then is how we treat people who cannot possibly do us any good. We can also refer to the "Golden Rule," by treating others the way we want to be treated. As previously stated, trust and empathy are both foundational pillars that demonstrate who a person is. From those tenets flow competency, trustworthiness, loyalty and humility that form all other guiding principles and core values. Conceptualizing the importance of motivation rather than power to form collaborations and partnerships to influence and synergize people can be transformational in addressing Substance Use Disorder. That was best illustrated by Dwight D, Eisenhower when he stretched out a string on a table. He said, "If you pull it, it will follow you anywhere, but if you try to push it, it will go nowhere" (https://www.brainyquote.com/quotes/dwight_d_eisenhower_149098). This could be a strong driver in approaching and influencing a specific course of action in terms of a person, an organization or a shared vision and decision-making while using active listening (Eddy, Lorenza, & Mastrangelo, 2008). With commonality of purpose we can endeavor for excellence where efforts are multiplied when people work together. It is then that you begin to understand that people are the real change agents. We must remember that all life has purpose and meaning that never ceases, (Dhiman 2011). With a firmness of heart and mind leaders can stand with those in the face of any adversity to confront the challenges before them. Today, one of our great challenges is Substance Use Disorder resulting from unlawful drug use. Many lives have been lost because of this epidemic. We are facing a new reality that may demand a different world view in meeting the challenge ahead. Doing the same thing resulting in the same outcome is one of the biggest obstacles in transformative change and facing up to the threat. Effective leaders know how to minimize resistance to change and generate momentum with the help of advocates in terms of the citizenry, public and private sector agencies. Confronting the brutal facts with an unwavering and steadfast faith is needed. We can look to the words of Prime Minister Winston Churchill during the darkest days of World War II with much of Europe and North Africa under Nazi control and where things seemed hopeless. He was convinced that even as bad as the situation was that Britain would ultimately prevail and is quoted as saying, "We are resolved to destroy Hitler or any of his gang. We shall fight him by land. We shall fight him by sea. We shall fight him in the air. Until, with God's help, we have rid the earth of his shadow" (Collins 2001). That is the kind of resoluteness and steady hand that is needed today. We can, and we are, making a difference!

REFERENCES

Collins, J. (2001). *Good to great.* NY, NY: HarperCollins Publishers, Inc.

Covey, S. R. (1991). *Principled centered leadership: the 7 habits of highly effective people.*

New York, New York: Free Press.

Dhim, S. (2011). Personal mastery and authentic leadership. *Organizational Development*

Journal, 29)2), 69-83, retrieved from http://search.proquest.com/docview/899227431? Accounted?=12085

Eddy, E. R., Lorenzet, S. J., & Mastrangelo, A. (2008). Personal and professional leadership in a government agency. *Leadership & Organization Development Journal, 29*(5), 412-426. doi:http://dx.doi.org/10.1108/01437730810887021.

Ratcliffe, J. H. (2003). *Intelligence-led policing:* Australian Institute of Criminology. Retrieved January 21, 2015 from http://search.proquest.com/docview/189398706?accounted=12085.

Warrick, D.D. (2011). The urgent need for skilled transformational leaders: Integrating transformational leadership and organization development. *Journal of Leadership, Accountability and Ethics, 8*(5), 11-26. Retrieved February 24, 2015 from http://search.proquest.com/docview/909486088?accountid=12085.

https://addiction.surgeongeneral.gov/sites/default/files/surgeon-generals-report.pdf

http://www.brainyquote.com/quotes/quotes/d/dwightdei149098.html

"SUBSTANCE USE DISORDER RESPECTS NO ONE"

DR CASTELLANO

It's been about 35 years that I have been practicing medicine in Elk County. During that time, I have witnessed numerous tragic deaths. I can remember vividly the first overdosed patient brought in by an ambulance. He was about 18 years old lying rigid on the stretcher with arms locked in a fixed position due to rigor mortis. His skin was mottled bluish- purple in color. That was around 1989 and only the beginning of the drug addiction epidemic.

Since then, numerous lives were destroyed leaving in its wake a trail of heartbreak that changed forever their families and friends. Many innocently started out on prescription meds and unknowingly became addicted, so much so, that they eventually resorted to buying drugs on the street. At one time I heard that Elk County had proportionally more heroin addicts per population than New York City.

"SUBSTANCE USE DISORDER RESPECTS NO ONE"

Substance Use Disorder (SUD) respects no one. I have seen so many professionals, doctors, nurses, policemen, businessmen, teachers all become addicted. Addiction is so powerful that the consequences are meaningless. Knowing that it will lead to a downhill spiral that the addict continues, unable to stop. I watched the addict's complete disregard of their responsibilities to family and their profession, ultimately throwing their life away. Many ended in suicide either by drugs or violent methods.

I did experience what I think was equal to the heroin high. It was when I was thirty years old and during a procedure the doctor gave me an IV narcotic. WOW! I couldn't believe the euphoria and peaceful state of mind. Nothing bothered me, not even the medical procedure that I was undergoing. I thought, if this is what addiction feels like it is no wonder that the habit is so hard to break. I thought it felt like I went to heaven, no worries, and the most peaceful feeling imaginable. When the procedure was done the doctor reversed the narcotic with Narcan. BAM! It was as if I got hit with a sledge hammer--- the return to reality was horrible. I will never forget that beautiful high and the abrupt withdrawal.

That experience gave me an insight to better understand SUD behavior and the powerful attraction to drugs. If you think about it, when an addict or alcoholic is overwhelmed with stress or heartbreak, they can magically eliminate the pain by getting high with alcohol or drugs. Unfortunately, it is just a temporary fix and life's stress will rear its ugly head again and again, fueling the addiction.

I read an article about addiction in which the author made a profound statement, one that I will never forget. He said, "god made one mistake by making opiate receptors." I thought about that and realized the power in the statement. How one system in our bodies can be so overwhelming that is could override the survival instinct. Even animals have opiate receptors. An experiment with monkeys had them insert an IV in each arm. One IV had glucose solution and the other morphine. The foot pedals controlled which IV solution would be administered. The monkeys chose the Morphine consistently, never once choosing the glucose solution. Which would have kept them alive. They chose the Morphine until it eventually killed them. Even the animal kingdom isn't immune to addiction, even their desire to get high overrides their instinct to survive. I am only sharing this so that you understand how powerful addiction can be.

I would like to give one last analogy. I think that the use of narcotics and sedatives are seductive, giving a warm and fuzzy feeling that no one can deny. It's like a baby tiger or bear cubs, loving and cuddly at first, allowing you to feel comfortable controlling them and responding to their affection. They're cute, but as they grow they get harder to handle and become more independent. Eventually, they're not so cute, and if you're not careful they will eat you alive. That's how addiction can start, slowly at first; little things, softer drugs, pot, prescription pills. They don't feel like much at first, they don't seem to have any real hold on you, but slowly, you try more, you want something stronger, some more powerful drugs, gradually losing self-control. Eventually the drugs become your master, and like the baby tiger and bear cubs, they are powerful enough to destroy you.

~ **Dr. Castellano**

"A PHARMACISTS JOURNEY OF UNDERSTANDING OPIOID USE DISORDER"

I read the book "Ripples - Effects of Addiction" cover to cover. I wrote an essay for Drug Topics, which is a national magazine for the community pharmacist, that was published in November 2021. https://www.drugtopics.com/view/ripple-effect-the-opioid-epidemic-challenges-even-the-most-resilient-communities

While reading this book, I saw several familiar names of people I grew up with. I graduated with Mary Levanduski, and her husband Buzzy who graduated a year after us. I unloaded Rudy Kocjancic's log truck in the wood yard in Johnsonburg's paper mill during my summer break. Patty Greene is the mother-in-law of my nephew Joe. I have read lots of articles on the impact of the opioid epidemic, but nothing hits harder than seeing names of people you grew up with.

I graduated from St. Marys Area High School in 1976, and enrolled in the University of Pittsburgh to study pharmacy. I graduated from Pitt's School of Pharmacy in 1981, and married my lab partner the same year. Denise and I started practicing community pharmacy in Clearfield, and after six months of working for Rite Aid, I had had enough of their staffing levels. We landed jobs in Blair County, where we worked for 38 years of our career. I worked at Kopp Drug for 26 years, and Thompson Pharmacy for 12 years. When we started working in 1981, a prescription for 60 Percocet (oxycodone/acetaminophen) meant someone was probably dying of cancer, and in extreme pain.

After the introduction of Oxycontin in the mid 1990's opioids became rather commonplace. As I practice today dispensing 120 Percocet on a monthly basis is all too routine. The physicians became too comfortable prescribing these pain meds, the pharmacists are all too comfortable dispensing them, the manufacturers are all too comfortable making them, the wholesalers are all too comfortable distributing them, and the patients are all too comfortable demanding and taking them. This being said prescriptions in the U.S. outside of hospitals for opioids fell about 44% in the eight years leading to 2020, while opioid overdose deaths nearly tripled in that time span, and increased even more in 2021. It is not the prescription opioids killing people, we all are acutely aware it is the fentanyl that is killing our people.

One of the biggest events in my career is when the DATA 2000 act became effective, which allows physicians to dispense buprenorphine as medication assisted treatment-MAT (better referred to as medication for opioid use disorder- MOUD). I was at Kopp Drug at the time, and dispensed Suboxone to less than half dozen patients. Initially I was not a fan, feeling like most pharmacists it was replacing one addictive substance for another. The analogy was to stop eating Whoppers, and start eating Big Macs.

Around 2008, my attitude took a 180 degree turn at the most unexpected place. My wife Denise, also a pharmacist, and I attended a drug promotional dinner for Seroquel-SR at Duffy's Tavern in Boalsburg, PA. It is our favorite restaurant, and even more a favorite when someone else is footing the bill. After the discussion about the antipsychotic Seroquel-SR, I started discussing Suboxone with Dr. Tim Derstine, one of the most brilliant psychiatrists I have ever met. I told him about my patients taking Suboxone, and asked him "why don't you doctors ever reduce the dose and get them off this drug?"

Dr. Derstine smiled and said "Pete, you are thinking like a pharmacist, and that is OK, because that is your training." I don't mean anything by that." He went on to say, "Taking a patient off Suboxone is not like taking them off a beta-blocker (heart drug) where you reduce the dose every two weeks. It is my job as a psychiatrist to figure out what made them stick that needle in their arm *the first time.*"

I felt like St. Paul being knocked to the ground on the way to Damascus (Acts 9:3-6). A two-minute conversation with this brilliant physician knocked me to the ground, and opened my eyes to what substance use disorder is, a mental health illness. We pharmacists are too focused on the mu receptors in the brain, and not on the mental health of the patient.

When I saw that Kopp Drug would be sold to Rite Aid, I needed to find another independent pharmacy. Thompson Pharmacy in Altoona fit that bill. I was assigned to the Broad Avenue location, probably the last place most pharmacists in Blair County would want to practice. It had a bad reputation that we worked hard to clean up. When I left Thompson pharmacy in 2020, every pharmacist wanted to practice there. We dispensed a lot of buprenorphine there, as many chains in Altoona would refuse to. I gained the respect and confidence of many of the patients with substance use disorder. I was their lifeline.

Dr. Rachel Levine, who now is the Assistant Secretary of Health for the federal government wrote the first standing orders on October 28, 2015 allowing pharmacists to dispense Naloxone without a prescription. At the Pennsylvania Pharmacists Convention in September 2016, she came to promote use of Naloxone. After she talked about the patients requesting this drug, I asked her if it is appropriate for pharmacists to initiate the discussion. She responded "God, I wish every pharmacist would do that." I took her advice to heart.

We took action, and immediately started dispensing Narcan® to all of our buprenorphine (Suboxone) patients. Even though they are in treatment, they can still "fall off the wagon." More importantly, they are still in those social circles where Narcan might save a life. The Center for Disease Control suggests that any patient taking more than 50 morphine milligram equivalents (MMEs) be given Naloxone (Narcan).

It was determined that buprenorphine is thirty times more potent than morphine. Therefore, most patients who are using Suboxone 8/2 twice a day (most common dose) are getting 480 Morphine milligram equivalents. To put it in their language, Suboxone 8/2 twice daily is equivalent to Oxycontin 80mg four times daily. Oxycodone is 1.5 times more potent than morphine. At Thompson Pharmacy I would dispense well over 150 Narcan kits a year. Three patients reported back to me that they used that medication to save someone's life.

I was also working two days a week at Dr. Zane Gates's office as his clinical pharmacist, and worked with a social worker from Blair County Drug and Alcohol program. With her connections, she got funding for four of us to earn an Opioid Treatment Specialist Certificate, through Clarion University. I completed this very extensive 12 credit course in March 2020. This also opened my eyes wider to the mental health aspects of substance use disorder.

My wife, Denise, and I moved to Morgantown WV to live closer to our oldest daughter and her husband, and precious grandson. I interviewed at Nickman's Drug store near Uniontown PA, and landed the job as Director of Clinical Services for his 5-store chain, which has locations in small towns in Fayette County. I immediately went to work with my Narcan promotion. We developed a flyer discussing the pharmacology of Narcan and buprenorphine. EVERY one of our Suboxone patients and anyone using more than 50 MME of any opioid gets Narcan and counseling. In two years at Nickman's, I have had 5 patients report back to me that they used the Narcan I dispensed to save someone's life.

The biggest struggle I see, is the prejudice of pharmacists dispensing these medications. I have had pharmacists and doctors tell me that Narcan encourages "Narcan Parties" and addicts pushing the dose to get higher. This is complete nonsense. I explain to these practitioners, that patients using opioids after a time use them to prevent withdrawal (dope sick), as opposed to getting high. Why would they want to experience acute withdrawal from Narcan, when the reason most continue to use opioids to prevent withdrawal? At a PAIN conference in Las Vegas, I explained just that to a physician from Oklahoma. He was more than grateful for my explanation... I felt like Dr. Derstine in 2008!

Whether in Altoona, PA, or Uniontown, PA, or across the nation, many pharmacists will not dispense buprenorphine products. In a study, 6,000 pharmacies were surveyed. Data from 4984 pharmacies (3402 chain and 1582 independent) were analyzed. Researchers found that both medications (Narcan and Suboxone) were available in 41.2 % of pharmacies, Suboxone was available in 48.3%, and Naloxone nasal spray was available in 69.5%. Only half of pharmacies audited would dispense buprenorphine 8/2 strips #14. Surprisingly enough, California had the lowest at 31% while Maine had 86% of the pharmacists who would dispense buprenorphine. About 1/5 pharmacies refused to order whatsoever. (https://www.sciencedirect.com/science/article/abs/pii/S0376871622002551?via%3Dihub). Sadly enough, my brother and sister pharmacists practicing independent community pharmacy were less likely to dispense buprenorphine. I am ashamed.

With headlines from NPR that read, **"DEA takes aggressive stance toward pharmacies trying to dispense addiction medicine."** (https://www.npr.org/sections/health-shots/2021/11/08/1053579556/dea-suboxone-subutex-pharmacies-addiction), I can't blame my colleagues for their lack of passion for dispensing buprenorphine. On one hand we have Health and Human Services wanting more doctors to prescribe more buprenorphine, especially in underserved areas like Elk County, while the DEA wants to "crack down on pharmacists who dispense buprenorphine." If two of the most influential governmental agencies (HHS and DEA) cannot agree, how on earth can we get more pharmacists and doctors to agree to help these desperate patients?

The DEA actively hassles pharmacies that dispense plain buprenorphine 8mg (Subutex®) tablets. They feel there is more abuse potential because of the lack of Naloxone. Many opioid experts disagree with the DEA stance. The DEA feels that the Subutex® has a higher likelihood of being diverted. When one really thinks about it, so what if it gets diverted? Who does it get diverted to? If you had a bucket full of Subutex® and you did not have substance use disorder, you would have no interest in taking this drug. Who does Subutex get diverted to? Heroin addicts. Is that a bad thing, that a heroin addict takes a medication that is a measured dose, that does not require injection, and has no chance of respiratory depression?

In spite of every pharmacist's concern about the DEA watching every pill we dispense, I feel obligated to help patients struggling with SUD. On my one-hour drive to work every day, I listen to morning Mass on YouTube. Last week, the priest read the Gospel of the Good Samaritan, and presented it with a unique interpretation. We've all heard the parable so I do not need to tell the story. What I found interesting is the priest mentioned the two religious men who walked by the man who was beaten up by the robbers. One was a "priest" and one was a "Levite" who walked on the other side of the road to avoid helping the fallen man. The Mass celebrant explained that the two men were more concerned about following the Jewish rules of purity, than they were helping the victim. The two religious men were not "bad men" they were simply following the rules of their religion.

I feel that many of the pharmacists I know are like the two religious men in the parable. They are too concerned about following what they perceive to be the rules, and are taking the "higher road." While they are being so righteous (in their own eyes), a lot of people are suffering.

I am 64 years old, and have been practicing pharmacy for over 40 years. I will probably stop practicing when I see this profession become more passionate about helping patients with SUD and other mental health disorders. We can do better as health care providers. I am passionate about helping my patients, whether it is monitoring blood sugar, taking seizure medications, giving COVID and flu shots, or keeping them alive with naloxone and buprenorphine. I only wish I would have been there for the Titchners, Kocjancics and Levanduskis.

~ **Peter Kreckel**

"THE LAST STEP"

It's just after midnight, the ringing phone pierces the night, waking me immediately, I'm a light sleeper. After all, it's been almost 12 years since I began this journey as the county coroner, and I've come to know the roads of this county better than most. However, my travels are always ones of sorrow, filled with sadness and despair for so many families.

I get up and get dressed, kissing my family lightly as I head out the door, making a mental note of what direction I'll take to get to your home. As I drive up to the house, it's not lost on me what I'm about to encounter. I know on the other side of that door I'll find another devastated family, another tragedy, another loss of a young life.

First comes the briefing from the police, then I'm escorted to your loved one. Sometimes their youth takes my breath away, sometimes the screams in the next room are so loud, it's deafening. The sounds and emotions of utter loss and devastation are raw and visceral, and something I'll never get used to. Sometimes the silence takes its own form, enveloping me in a reality that's all too familiar for some. I then must ask the hard questions, the uncomfortable ones. I never mean to appear insensitive, but part of my job entails determining both the cause and manner of death. Doing so means asking the delicate questions…how long has your loved one struggled with addiction? When is the last time you saw them alive? Did you notice anything different in their behavior over the last few days or weeks? Sometimes families are very forthcoming with their story, other times not so much. Some have known deep down that eventually this day may come, while other times the family truly didn't know their loved one even experimented with drugs. Then there are the times when I watch your small children stare at me with wide eyes, scared and unsure why all these people are in their home. I watch their grandparents struggle to tell them that their mommy or daddy went to heaven and isn't coming back. The looks on their small, innocent faces are the ones that haunt me the most. As a parent myself, my heart breaks for each family.

What never changes is the hurt. It seems to pour from every orifice. It never gets any easier to stand in front of a distraught mother or father and explain how their child died.

Be it overdose, intentional or unintentional, the hurt and despair remains the same. I've stood in the homes of countless families over the years, always the uninvited and unwelcomed guest. To a few I'm the enemy, but I'm okay with that. Grief takes strange forms, and I don't pretend to know what it's like to have someone tell you that your child is gone. But I can empathize and offer a helping hand. What you may or may not know about me is that your loved one isn't just a drug death to me. I'm acutely aware that this person who lays before me is somebody's someone. A daughter, a friend, a grandson, the neighbor kid, the rock of the family…and the list goes on.

Having been down this road more times than I can recall, I am overtly aware of the carnage that is left in the wake of a death from Drugs. I am also aware of the dark stigmas and generalizations that many associate with drug addiction. Yet, I don't think someone's struggle with addiction makes them a bad person. We all have crosses to bear, some heavier than others. Addiction doesn't make you a bad person, it makes you a person with a medical condition, oftentimes also complicated by depression, anxiety, and a host of other mental health conditions. Through the many years that I have been coroner, I've come to understand that addiction is a cold and lonely road. It is a struggle that takes over and completely changes someone, and in far too many cases, is what eventually kills them.

The days eventually turn to weeks and months. I run into your family from time to time, sometimes at the grocery store, sometimes at the death of another child. Some offer a smile and hug, and others turn their eyes downward and keep walking. I understand, I really do. I know I serve as a painful reminder of the worst day of their lives, and if they can't bear to talk with me, that's okay.

I've been a funeral director for longer than I've been the coroner, so I see the funeral side of these stories as well. I've always said that when someone young dies, we are burying the future. All the hopes for graduations, weddings, a clean and sober life, or maybe a certain aspiration. I once sat with a mother who held both of my hands as she cried and shared that her daughter had once had dreams of becoming a funeral director like myself. I always wish could take away their pain, but we all know that isn't possible. What I can do is pray for you, pray for your family, and pray for peace, comfort, and a flooding of fond memories to help you through these dark days...

~ Michelle Muccio, Coroner and Funeral Director~

FINAL THOUGHTS

Loss, sorrow, pain, and joy. All of the things we go through. My loss is great, losing my beautiful son, but my joy is greater that I got the gift of being his mother. The outcome was painful and broke my heart, he made my life so hard at times. The endless worry, the sleepless nights, begging and praying for some divine intervention to save him. Was it to save him, or was my prayer to save me?

I was tired, hurt, betrayed, and beaten down. I had already lost so much, I just wanted him to be better. I wanted him to be that beautiful little boy that I laughed with, tickled, made cookies with, hide-n-seek, and rocked to sleep to come back to me, to be whole, normal. After all, I loved him so very much. But was it a selfish thing on my part? Did I want him to be something he just wasn't able to be? I don't know. Of course, as I saw it and many of us who have an addict as a loved one want what we think is best for them. We want them to be everything. We want them to live up to our expectations. However, maybe that isn't something he wanted, maybe that isn't something he could do, maybe that wasn't his journey here? I don't have the answers; I only have the questions. I wanted my suffering to end as much as I wanted him to have the happy life that I thought he should have, that, in my eyes, he deserved! Isn't if sad when our child exceeds? We are so proud of them, but we are also thinking somewhere in the back of our heads, Good job! And then when they fail, we feel like failures, esp. when it comes to addiction. We want to curl up in that same dark hole they live in. We failed them somehow, it has to be our fault, right? Or we distance ourselves from them because we feel shame and guilt. We have our own "stinking thinking," as my dear friend would tell me.

Did my suffering end when he died? No, I was given a life sentence of guilt, sorrow, and longing. My heart hurt so bad at times I wondered how in the world did it go on beating? Why did I keep waking up in the morning? Why did the world keep on spinning? Damn it! Why couldn't I just get off somewhere? Did I not have enough in my life? Breast cancer, losing two infants, abuse, and much, much more. Guess not. I had no control over any of it. Day after day I would wake up praying it was a nightmare, praying for some kind of do over.

FINAL THOUGHTS

I would cry out: "Please, lord, let me have one more hour with him, let me say all the things I didn't say, let me warn him, please, lord, just let me have a do-over." Sad thing is, there is no do-over.

I wanted to know why my life was so hard? What did I do to deserve this? But this wasn't about me. It was about him. This was his choice, his battles.

Then sweet Kelly gave me a letter that changed me forever. It was a letter from Danny that he had written a good year or more before he passed away.

Danny wrote "If addiction kills me, don't grieve for me, but use me to help others" The gauntlet was thrown down, this was his last wish that I had right in front of me in black n white. I whispered quietly,

"Honey, I will" it also followed with, "But I can't promise you that I will not grieve for you the rest of my life."

So, my journey began.

Danny's death consumed me, and I wanted to save all the Danny's and the Danielle's in the world. I wanted to save the mothers, fathers, sisters, brothers, and children from the pain of this senseless death.

I started to reach out to people who I knew who were in recovery to help me understand this tremendous pull on them, I need to understand a little more than I did. Yes, Danny and I talked about it, but I was always afraid to ask "those" hard questions. A very dear friend of mine asked me if I had ever heard of the phrase chasing the dragon? I had, but not in the content he was referring to.

He told me that they are always looking to feel the first high, and they continue to chase the dragon to get that. He also explained that when people referred to a "bad bunch of heroin," that was what they all flocked to, they wanted to achieve that ultimate high again. I sat there at the picnic table with my dear friend while he went on and explained to me the mind of an addict. Even though this was early after Danny's death, I understood a little more. He was not the first one I talked to, and he wasn't to be the last.

My search began for me to have a better understanding. You may or may not get this, but with more knowledge came more guilt. Why didn't I talk to Danny more? Why didn't I ask these hard questions? I struggled with those emotions, and I was alone in my thoughts. I would feel so alone at times. I was angry, I was angry at the world. I had this burden to carry, and I didn't feel safe enough to share these dark thoughts. I couldn't show weakness.

Then I started pounding the pavement, trying to bring more awareness to this growing epidemic, I did all kinds of things to shake people out of this coma they resided in. This is real! This can be your kid; this can be a loved one! I tried to spend more time with the younger kids and tell them my story. And all the time, I was trying to maintain a normal life. Ugh. I felt trapped inside.

FINAL THOUGHTS

More kids kept dying, and everyone I heard about I would weep; it was like it was happening to me again. I knew the heartache, the pain.

But after 22 years with Danny's addiction and 8 years since he has been gone (May 18,2014), I am still watching these kids take that first dose and sometimes their last, I am still watching people struggle with this monster, demon. Watching some of these kids that played ball with him, watching friends of mine as their loved ones go down that rabbit hole.

I have to ask, what is the answer? What do we do?

I am by far not an authority on this. I am just a mom who loved her son with all her heart and wanted to save him.

Stigma is a problem, yes, but there are also many other things. Convincing them there is hope, convincing others not to pretend it will go away and understand, Yes, it can be your kid. It can be anybody's kid or loved one. We love people through cancer and other illnesses, yet why is it hard to understand how we can love them through addiction?

When you get your child into counseling, may I recommend you get some too. It is a family disease. It ruins marriages, ruins relationships, it pulls families apart. It leaves open wounds on everyone it touches, and sometimes these wounds don't heal.

But the ugly of some of it when they were here with us was just as hard—hiding everything that could be sold for drugs, stealing, and lying. The manipulation to the point that we questioned everything we did. They break our self-confidence; they shake our world to the core. It breaks us as parents. It causes a deep slash inside our souls. We fight with people we love to defend the addict, we fight with anyone and everyone that questions us about our child. And yet, we continue to try to maintain some kind of life, we go to work, we do all the daily duties, yet inside we are always wondering,

"is he ok?" "is he alive? Where is he?"

Along with, what can I do? What did I miss? What could I do differently? We are trapped inside our head, and the only people that understand are the same ones that are going through it when they are brave enough to open up and let others know. You talk about loneliness; you have no idea how a parent feels in the face of their child's addiction.

Danny comes to visit me in my dreams. He leaves me guitar picks in random places. He brings people into my life. He gave me peace. Saying that, don't think I am ok. I still cry in the car by myself. I still lay awake at night and thinking about him. Even though I know better, I still tell him about his amazing daughter, all the beautiful nieces and nephews, and all the things I feel he is missing. I also know that he is releasing me from the fight. It may be time to pass the torch on.

Danny and God let me know that he is free. That they were sorry that I had to endure such heartache, but Danny, my sweet little mud monster, was free of the demons that plagued him. The monkey on his back and that pain in his soul, he was free. They were sorry.

If you have lost someone, please know they are there with you. Loving you just as much as they did when they were here. They don't want you to be sad, and I know how hard that can be. But Danny's death and a few other things that have happened made me understand death a lot differently. Live your life to the fullest and do things they would want to do. That is the way to honor them and keep them alive. Do it with joy.

May God bless all of you as much as I feel blessed.

~Patricia Greene

I WANT TO THANK

My very amazing niece Kate, I don't have enough words to express my gratitude to this fantastic lady. I am truly blessed. She is always there to lend a hand, contribute her time and lets me bounce ideas off of her. She has always been there for me no matter what I want to do. Without her support so many things would have never happened.

My Beautiful Children:

Cassie, who is thoughtful and always willing to help me when I get stuck, as my daughter she has greatly inspired me, however, she is an amazing person all the way around. I am blessed to be her mom

Nick, the most tender and kind heart, I am so lucky to be his mom. He has such talent; I am sure one day; he will write an amazing story of his own. Once he gets started..

My dear sweet Amy, you have been such an amazing person in my life. How many times have I turned to you, and you always have time for me. All your positive words when I was ready just to quit. I hit the lottery the day we became family.

FAMILY:

My Dear Sister Carol, you have picked me up and brushed me off more times than I can count. Thank you for helping raise me. You are the lioness there to always protect me.

My Brother Steve, for the millions of questions, for the millions of phone calls, for rooting me on, for your positive encouragement, and for knowing just what I need to hear to make me feel better. I couldn't ask for a better brother, even if you did cut the heads off my dolls to make your movie! UGH!

My sister in law Susan, you always believed in me. I remember so many talks we had and use to tell me I could do anything. I just had to believe in myself first. You were right.

For my other daughter Tarah, for offering your words of encouragement and never forgetting me, for bringing Esme into our world. What a gift she is.

My mother-in-law, Anona, who always tells me what I am doing is important and how proud of me she is and loves me no matter what.

I WANT TO THANK

FRIENDS:

My dear friends Marsha and Sharon who are like sisters to me, they let me vent, and always take my side. You have been there when good times weren't.

Cyndi Muccio, for helping, guiding, loving, and being there at all times of the day. God has made us sisters. You continue to give me hope and help me find my light again. I am so blessed to have you in my life.

To everyone who wrote and helped me pull this together, with only one goal in mind, to make a difference, each story was written with love and determination to help someone else. Your unselfish acts will help save many. Without your heartfelt testimonies, this would have never been possible. I harped and pestered many of you because I knew you had something important to say. It wasn't by chance; it was divine intervention.

Kate McGonnell, you don't know how much I admire you. When things were so hard, you were always there to lend a helping hand or guide me in the right direction. Lord knows I need it! And then help me with all the final touches. What a gift you are.

Lisa Mancuso, I cannot express what your friendship has meant. You always make time to help me, answer questions, and be there for me. Your acts of kindness have had a "Ripple" effect. Tyler would be so proud of his mama. Continue to make many more "smiles". Thank you for your contribution to book one and book 2. You truly have a gift for seeing beauty.

To Ken, who is there and willing to give me a hug when I need one. Thank you for distracting me when I am stubborn and won't take a break.

All My MOMS Know how much I love each one of you and how very important you are to me.

For all the people who have stopped me in the store, sent me messages, wrote me letters, or sent me a card. Know how important all your acts of kindness have meant to me and all your positive comments.

I have had so many things happen in my life, but each one of you came and helped me piece my life together. You never know how important those words of kindness or encouragement are. When I was at my lowest point, all of you picked me back up.

To my 814 generation kids, you will always have a piece of my heart. You all inspired me to make a difference.

I have one last Acknowledgement.

I am so grateful for the unconditional love you have taught me., for the people you have put into my path to love me, help me and guide me, I would have crumbled and disappeared without you by my side. You never gave up on me. You were there in my darkest times; even when I thought you had abandoned me and left me alone to stumble in the darkness, you were there. You were the soft whisper in my heart, the gentle nudge at my soul. You were with me in the middle of the night when I was afraid and full of doubt and fear. You came to comfort me. I know I would have never made it this far without you.

You are my source of strength and love.

Thank you, my dear heavenly Father. I am humbly your servant.

~Patricia Greene~